P S Y
REGR

60447802090100

8510

0044789264352

8705

PSYCHO REGRESSION

A New System for Healing & Personal Growth

Dr. Francesca Rossetti

SAMUEL WEISER, INC.

York Beach, Maine

First published in the United States in 1994 by
Samuel Weiser, Inc.
Box 612
York Beach, Maine 03910

99 98 97 96 95 94
9 8 7 6 5 4 3 2 1

Library of Congress Catalog Card Number: 93-40634

ISBN 0-87728-788-0
BJ

Cover illustration by Ananda Kurt Pilz, from The Walter
Holl Agency, Germany.

Typeset in Baskerville

Printed in the United States of America

The paper used in this publication meets the minimum re-
quirements of the American National Standard for Perma-
nence of Paper for Printed Library Materials Z39.48-1984.

**THIS BOOK IS DEDICATED TO MY
HOLY GUARDIAN ANGEL**

Also to all of those who think they know, those who know they
do not know, and to those who are wanting and willing
to know themselves . . .

CONTENTS

ACKNOWLEDGMENTS

My sincere thanks to all of the extraordinary people that I have been fortunate enough to meet through the years and who have helped me in different ways, directly and indirectly, to unfold this very sacred therapy.

I appreciate those who are now deceased for being who they were, and also the ones alive today
Not forgetting all of the patients who have helped me to gain a greater insight

His Holiness Shri Ram Chandra, Master of the Sahaj Marg System of Meditation, India
His Holiness The Dalai Lama, Dharmasala, India
The Ven Stavira Sangharakshita, Buddhist, England
Geoffrey Watkins, Watkins Books, England
Bishop Francis Forsyth, Pre-Nicene Catholic Church, England
Bishop Richard Palatine, Pre-Nicene Catholic Church, England
Canon Andrew Glazewski, Roman Catholic, Devon

Dr Mark L. Gallert, radionics, USA

Joseph Rael, Beautiful Painted Arrow, shaman/healer, USA

Twylah Nitsch, Seneca Indian, Wolf Clan, spiritual teacher, USA

Bernice (Falling Leaves) Hucole, native American teacher, USA

Dr Bob Ramirez, MD parasitologist, USA

Master Otaki Sensei, Samurai Shinto Master, Japan

Sam Lono, Kahuna, Hawaii

David Menongye, Hopi sand painter and tribal elder, USA

Kuzungu, healer and witchdoctor, Kenya

Odilon da Silva, psychic surgeon, Brazil

Professor Santiago Americano Freire, MD, psychiatrist and scientist, Brazil

Josephine Sisson, psychic surgeon, Philippines

Virgilo Gutierrez, psychic surgeon, Philippines

David Oligane, exorcist/psychic surgeon, Philippines

Bishop Victor Dane, The Holy Orthodox Catholic Apostolic Church of the East, USA

George Alexander, spiritual teacher and healer, England

And 'If the last should be first'...

Frances Tweed-Clarke, RGN, manager, qualified masseuse, England. With deep appreciation for spending many hours correcting and typing the manuscript. Also for formulating the Glossary.

To: Judy Piatkus, Piatkus Books, who gave me the incentive to write again after a fifteen year gap, during which time I was involved in healing, travelling and research.

Also to all of my invisible helpers and friends who have helped me, and continue to help me to spiritually assimilate the information acquired (throughout those years) with the inner knowledge which continues to be channelled through me regarding this work.

THE AUTHOR'S JOURNEY TO THE BIRTH OF PSYCHO-REGRESSION

During my early childhood I had a number of unusual experiences and I became aware at a very young age that I had my own personal Guardian Angel. This knowledge was very reassuring. In my childhood my Guardian Angel saved me from being trampled by a horse which was out of control. My Guardian Angel also spoke to me in the presence of my father when we were saying evening prayers. During my school years in a convent, I was quite mystified as to why words like 'sin', 'hell' and 'purgatory' seemed to come up a lot in religious instruction. I was aware that God is the God of love, so this did not make sense to me. I felt quite sorry for the nuns when they blushed at the mention of the word 'sex'; I knew that they were trying to talk about something which they did not really understand. This caused great confusion when they were not able to express the difference between the Immaculate Conception and human sexual love. During religious instruction we were told that Jesus was not conceived through 'normal channels', but the nuns were not prepared to tell us what these normal channels were.

In my early teens I became strongly aware that God was not an old man in the sky. I had the thunderous realisation that He was in fact within me. This came as a great shock. It took me quite a while to become accustomed to this new way of being, though it took me many years even to begin to understand the true nature of that revelation as this was contrary to orthodox Catholic teachings.

My father often talked to me over afternoon tea about the mysteries of the universe, and it was during this time that the doctrine of reincarnation made absolute sense to me, he talked so naturally about it. My mother also understood reincarnation to be an essential part of the soul's growth experience and she, too, often discussed this with me.

I had many interesting jobs in my early working years. For example, I worked in a Buddhist monastery in London, where I helped to compile a Buddhist magazine and wrote religious articles in Buddhist terminology. People then began to think that I was a Buddhist, not realising that I was simply a student of life.

Several years later I became manageress of the anti-quarian section of J. Watkins Bookshop, one of the main mystical, spiritual, religious bookshops in London. I met a lot of interesting people during this time and learnt about many different ways of walking the spiritual path.

I then trained for eight years with spiritual teacher Bishop Richard Palatine, who was a Christian mystic as well as a Gnostic. He taught me to have absolute reliance on the God-within and the importance of spiritual purification. Through his disciplinary training I began to understand myself a little better and realised just how brainwashed I had been. I learnt to become inwardly a lot stronger, more peaceful and self-reliant. I became interested in different religious beliefs and ideologies, and in different forms of spiritual purification and healing methods.

Many of my friends at that time were saving their money to take out mortgages, whereas I was putting every pound into travelling in order to expand my spiritual knowledge. I was generally considered by my family and friends to be far too idealistic and a dreamer. I had no understanding of the business world and the goal of material security, this did not mean anything to me. I just needed to travel to broaden my knowledge and awareness. My investment was being made with the God-within.

I used to get strong urges to visit different parts of the world, and when the feelings became very strong, I somehow managed to get there. I had a very deep connection with the American Indians and visited America half a dozen times. The Indian medicine people and shaman were very friendly and open towards me as they knew intuitively that I was wanting seriously to learn as much as I could in order to help my healing work.

I was given ceremonial rattles, sweet grass, beads and a ceremonial wand for healing and purification. I was taken through a seven-hour cleansing marathon by Joseph Rael (he is a shaman and visionary) in a ceremonial kiva in New Mexico, where I experienced life and death and felt the presence of my Indian ancestors helping me. Joseph told me that the healing had first to come from within. Various clues were given to me on how to accomplish this, although there was no structured system of healing.

During another visit to America, Senneca Indian Twylah Nitsch initiated me into the Wolf Clan. She knew inwardly that I had been an Indian before, and that I was there to reconnect with old links in order to help my healing work.

My quest for knowledge continued for many years, during which time I wanted to share this knowledge that I had acquired through my meetings with spiritual teachers, healers, shamans and paranormal researchers. Healing information was also channelled through me, usually after a major journey when a period of germination followed each trip, during which time I meditated and reflected on all that I had learnt and gradually this took form as I integrated it into my healing work. I then began to give talks. and seminars to small groups of people interested in spiritual subjects, later travelling to other countries giving lectures and seminars as the demand for the work grew.

When I was in Hawaii, Kahuna priest Sam Lono gave me a sacred healing stone and he also consecrated me as a healer in recognition of my work. And when lecturing in Japan I met Master Otake Sensei, the head of the Shinto School of Martial Arts in Tokyo. He initiated me into the healing section of the martial arts for my perseverance, determination and his recognition of the warrior within me.

I have also visited India, Greece, Thailand, the Philippines, Germany, East Africa, Egypt, Brazil, Peru, Finland, Turkey, Italy, Spain, Jamaica and Barbados. My quest for spiritual and healing knowledge has never dimmed.

I realised over the years that I was born with the unusual gift of being able to tune into different types of energy, using it for specific purposes connected with the work. The American Indian knowledge and energy helped me with the healing, enabling me consciously to energise myself through connecting with the spirit of earth, water, fire and air. The Indian energy within also helped me to connect with two-legged, four-legged and winged beings. This stirred within me knowledge and memories connected with other lives which I thought had long been forgotten, helping me to integrate my inner knowledge in order to expand the healing work. The Hawaiian energies strengthened me also, helping me to realise that I was not alone in my quest for wholeness. The Hawaiians knew about the great, giant-like spirit beings which inhabit the mountains and volcanoes, and they were aware that there really is an energy that resides within every life form which has the right to be reverenced.

The Japanese energy also stirred up past life memories, helping me to strive towards greater clarity of vision and directness. When I connected to the Japanese energy again in this life, I received a great deal of help to exorcise spirits, ghosts and demons through my spiritual connection with the Shinto ancestral energies.

Throughout all of these countries to which I travelled, the people involved in deeper aspects of healing recognised me as a valid researcher into the paranormal aspects of the human psyche, and today I am known as such, also as a spiritual teacher and healing channel. A number of years ago I wrote a book on exorcism which was well accepted; for this and all of my research into exorcism and unusual aspects of healing I received from the Universal Life Church in North America an honorary degree of Doctor of Divinity. I was also granted a Doctor of Divinity by the Pre-Nicene Catholic Church, UK. After training in the priesthood for eight years I was subsequently ordained.

When I was in India, I met His Holiness the Dalai Lama, The Grand Lama of Tibet, who presented me with the customary sacred white scarf (representing peace and purity). I was very aware of his charismatic and loving energies, and left with tears of joy and the knowledge that I had met a soul who really was able genuinely to communicate through the power of unconditional love.

I also had the privilege of meeting His Holiness Shri Ram Chandra, a well-known Indian of the Sahaj Marg system of meditation. He strongly recommended that I keep a record of my 'discoveries', so I followed his good advice and recorded as much as I possibly could on audiotapes. I became one of his pupils of his system of meditation, which when translated means 'Natural Path'. It is a powerful as well as a valid way of working on the releasing of negative karma without necessarily going through regression. The more contemplative type of person may prefer to follow this method of self-awareness. I continued to follow the Sahaj Marg system of meditation, as well as pursue my own researches into multi-dimensional healing.

Throughout the years, I became very busy with my healing work and survival, and with the process of integrating and evolving a new healing system. This I have called Psycho-Regression, because through this therapy, healing can take place within the mind, emotions, the body and the spirit.

My work now involves teaching, lecturing and continuing to carry out research into more paranormal aspects of the human psyche, as well as acting as a spiritual channel for transmissions to take place. These transmissions are connected with the Sahaj Marg system of meditation which releases group karma. I am also involved in sacramental healing.

Now I realise that time is accelerating and it is vital to put some of my tested ideas and discoveries (together with the inner knowledge that comes to me from other dimensions of reality), into book form in order to help as many people as possible from all walks of life, especially those who are interested in the deep and fascinating mysteries of the human psyche.

INTRODUCTION

Psycho-Regression is an unusual book inasmuch as it describes a totally new system of healing that takes place at very deep levels within the psyche. This book reveals systematically how it is possible to find the primal cause or causes of a problem that may have its roots buried thousands of years ago. This is the first time that such a succinct system of healing has been written about in the Western world and in such depth. Even within the last decade much of this information would still have been considered esoteric; in the ancient mystery schools of Greece and Egypt it would only be for initiates or the chosen few.

Psycho-Regression is not only about a new system of healing, it is also about the inner side of life. When you read this book you will discover that it can be used like a mirror to reveal different views of your own reflection, enabling you to understand the reasons for your actions more clearly and what it is that really motivates and moves you deeply, and why.

During the last 20 years of my researches some important information and knowledge has evolved helping to create this multi-dimensional healing system. We now know that it is possible to heal as well as to integrate our karma (or fate, as determined by the law of cause and effect concerning our actions and reactions from previous existences, as well as the result of our actions in this present lifetime).

Psycho-Regression will help you to understand the negative as well as the positive side of your nature far more clearly, from a non-intellectual point of view. We all have beautiful, positive energies which can be blocked by negativity, and once this is released and integrated through the therapy you most certainly will become a more vital and creative being.

You do not have to belong to a monastery, an orthodox religion or religious sect in order to bring about inner change. Most of us are working hard in the everyday world, endeavouring to earn a living and to spread a little happiness, but many of us also have a desire to discover the inner meaning of life, and this book, has the answers to many questions that you may not have been able to formulate consciously.

Psycho-Regression therapy is important in helping you to find the answers, as also is prayer, meditation, fresh air, a balanced diet, exercise, music, creativity, the sun, moon and stars. Releasing negative emotions such as past hurts, grief and anger helps us to appreciate the beauty around us more easily. We become 'lighter' and more aware when we are less burdened by the negative parts of ourselves. We also become far more sensitively attuned and are able to look into another person's eyes and to understand their needs, perhaps empathising with their hopes and dreams, and endeavouring to help these things to become reality.

We are also able to find out what is really creating the negativity or the hell within us. On understanding this and acknowledging our negativity, coupled with a desire to change, we can then clear out this negative karma, giving us a lot more room to discover our true potential and power. Gradually we become able to uncover who we really are, discovering the greatest mystery of all – ourselves.

The therapy is called Psycho-Regression because it treats the whole person, including the mind, the emotions, the spirit and the body. Through releasing all the negative emotions, the physical body gradually becomes stronger, thereby preventing dis-ease from becoming disease. A person who comes for Psycho-Regression therapy is first made to feel really secure in a pleasant environment and, after relaxing on a couch and listening to soft music, they are very gently taken into a deeper state of relaxation which enables their inner self to travel back in time in order to understand the origins of the main source of their problem.

It should be stressed that there is no hypnosis involved in this therapy. Rather, I use guided visualisation, which is more like daydreaming in pictures. Initially it may seem just like wild imaginings, until you slowly start to realise that you are reacting very strongly to what you perhaps first considered to be just a flight of fancy. With guided visualisation you are in control and can stop your experience at any time and within seconds, whereas hypnosis keeps the person controlled within the frame of their experience.

Re-living moments in past lives isn't painful or distressing. Most of the time you feel quite objective although you can feel quite tired or emotional after a session, [but] you can also feel very happy and relaxed. There is a great feeling of relief about resolving these issues which have been hanging around for thousands of years.

Woman *magazine article, April 1992*

A number of books have been written purely about regression, recounting many experiences of people reliving early childhood or past life traumas. Some of the material that surfaces during such experiences can enable a person to understand the reasons for their inner fears that may govern this present lifetime, which can be fascinating as well as illuminating. However, this only just reveals the tip of the iceberg within the human psyche which is very much deeper than one could ever intellectually comprehend, as it encompasses a wide range of past experiences and conditions associated with many un-resolved weaknesses and emotions.

Psycho-Regression therapy is very different from pure regression therapy as it releases and transforms negative energies, enabling you to connect with your true self. We all need to look for our own unique Holy Grail, or to find the God within us and Psycho-Regression therapy is able to help you to do this. When Michelangelo created the figure of David he inwardly saw the form etched within the rough stone. All he needed to do was to chisel away the unwanted pieces. The same principle applies to this sacred healing (called sacred because the healing is divinely motivated). The negative energies that block your power are gradually transmuted. The healing process can be a true work of art, enabling you to connect to the heart of God and integrating that essence within you.

If you are just nosy or simply curious and feel that you do not have any negativity, then regressing into parts of your hidden self will at the very least be inwardly satisfying. However, if something in your life particularly upsets you, then the first question you are likely to ask is, 'Why?' You may tremble or shudder when you see a mouse, a spider, a snake, an angry man or woman, or maybe feel emotional when you see a transient sunset, a flower in bloom, the happiness of lovers or a child crying, and your emotional reaction strongly suggests that what you are experiencing has been triggered by something much deeper within you. You cannot question all of your reactions, of course, or you would not be living life in the moment, but these emotions that affect you should at least be reflected upon. And if they disturb you deeply then Psycho-Regression can be a way of understanding the situation behind the outer circumstances, as well as releasing the negativity and filling the void with divine energy.

Deeply buried memories reside within our cellular structure and are locked within us. The body can be likened to a computer, storing all memories within the cells of the body and the aura (the subtle emanation around the physical body). This information can be recalled at any time, provided the right sequence of buttons is pressed in order for the correct information to be released. If used skilfully Psycho-Regression therapy has the ability to recall programmed information, releasing the non-essentials and negative emotions, then flooding the area with positive divine energy and colour in order for a new internal programme to be stored. This whole process is divinely directed according to the free will of the person being regressed. It is a very ritualised and systematic form of therapy, not an intellectual experience. The angels (see page 12) are able to work freely within this system, helping to transform the whole psyche.

Even if you do not undergo the therapy yourself, this book will give you a clear idea of what karma really is and how we are affected by it in our everyday lives. You can then integrate and become one with this knowledge through your own personal insight and it will make you more aware, enabling you to change your negative attitudes about yourself and life around you.

The therapy has evolved through me, with the help of my Guardian Angel, with direct assistance from the inner planes, and from the teachings and help of shamans, spiritual teachers and medicine people all over the world.

Through Psycho-Regression I am able to take people on an inner journey to the source of their problem, so that they understand what is really troubling them and not what they *think* is troubling them. This problem could be a negative experience which had occurred in this life, in early childhood or in a past incarnation. The negative emotions connected with the past events are then released. This is done with the help of the angels and other divine presences. An angel is a spiritual being that is able to draw off and transform negative energy on a psychic/spiritual level, helping a person to heal themselves. Angels are referred to in the Bible and in all religions as divine intermediaries between God and man. There are many different types of angels that help us in our everyday lives, including our own personal Guardian Angel who is with us 24 hours a day and for the whole of our life.

I do not heal people; I act as a channel to instigate the flow of divine power through the therapy in order for their energy to move. I work with the angels and spiritual guides, and the knowledge that flows through me. I have an inner knowing and the action that I should take is impressed upon my subconscious, so it is not always possible for me to explain every detail intellectually. I do not expect every reader to have the same perception and knowing; however, many of you will be able to feel the meaning and the understanding behind the words, thereby linking you into other dimensions of reality.

12

Psycho-Regression is not just another therapy; it encompasses so much more, enabling us to understand our beginnings and revealing many unusual aspects of ourselves. It helps us to understand how, through our past actions, we came to create the very structure of our being as we are today. We not only carry within us a physical genetic structure, but a psychic one as well. This psychic-genetic structure is the very essence of our karma which resides within every part of us and the negative side of this can be changed through this in-depth method of healing.

We also need to understand completely why we create our own personal infernos. If you seem to be going through some type of hell then you need to look deep within yourself to find out why this is happening. You cannot blame other people or difficult circumstances. We have to take responsibility for our own actions. Dr Carl Jung said many times that the outer world is a reflection of the inner self. Therefore, there is no one to blame, and nowhere to run and hide. We have to confront the problem face to face, and then have the courage to deal with it.

We need to understand thoroughly what karma is all about before we can clear it through Psycho-Regression, so this is explained in detail in Chapter 3.

Some healers are aware that injuries which may have occurred thousands of years ago can still be located within the psyche, causing areas of weakness within the present physical body. Through Psycho-Regression therapy these psychic injuries can be healed with the help of the angels and one's own divine self. This book is the first in which psychic injuries have been written about in such detail.

This book will take you into many hidden aspects of truth which are more amazing than the best science fiction (fact often being a lot stranger than fiction), especially in this type of healing. Parts of our spirit can actually be trapped in other time zones, and Chapter 6 looks at this phenomenon and explains how the trapped parts of the self can be released.

In Chapter 7 you will also discover some of the sources of sexual trauma, and how these can be worked out through sexual regression, which is a branch of Psycho-Regression therapy.

Chapter 8 is devoted to some unusual psychic discoveries, for example surrogate regression and the psychic aspects of blood transfusions.

In the latter part of this book (in Chapter 9) I discuss sub-personalities and how they can affect our lives in the present time. I will explain how it is possible to release the negative aspects of the past personality and enhance the positive in order to bring about a better integration of the true self.

When all the negative past energies have been transmuted it is then possible for us to discover who we really are. We are then able to connect with our primal powers (see Chapter 10), thus creating a luminous body that is no longer blocked with past negative emotions.

This book will give you essential information pointing you in the right direction, to make you more aware of some subtle aspects of your being which may have gone unnoticed before. It will not teach you how to be a therapist or shaman, since you would have to complete a highly specialised training course for this. People wishing to learn this therapy need to be intuitive and able spontaneously to flow with and assimilate information very quickly. They also need to be dedicated, patient and have plenty of physical stamina. Individuals wishing to practise this type of therapy need to work without any personal judgement, which is a tall order, but the opportunity is there for those who seek to work in depth with the human psyche. One of my aims in this life is to be able to teach people to become Psycho-Regression therapists in order to help individuals throughout the world. In order to be able to do this work you need to have a deep understanding of the natural laws that govern everyday life. These natural laws are simple and make spiritual as well as logical common sense. When these laws are broken either through ignorance or lack of thought it usually causes chaos for everyone involved.

For example, if one conceives a child in a drunken stupor or in lust, the wrong type of energy is created, allowing the child's spirit to be too vulnerable to negative external influences, which can cause many kinds of problems including spirit possession. If a growing child is constantly exposed to parental hate and anger, it will naturally be affected, carrying these negative parental emotions within its psyche. If a young girl is misinformed about menstruation or childbirth, this could bring about a fearful or painful experience. If sex is talked about as dirty and wrong, or referred to as basic or carnal, then a child brought up in this environment will grow up conditioned by this and may not be able to enjoy a harmonious sexual relationship.

Through understanding and assimilating the knowledge contained in this book it is possible to become aware of the limitless dimensions contained within the human psyche.

1
PSYCHIC-GENETICS

The understanding of psychic-genetics
as opposed to physical-genetics

The creation

In the beginning was God, the source of infinite, unmanifested energy. From within this great expanse of non-form, the seeds of unconditional love gradually ripened. Quite naturally the birth of love began to manifest, and God created heaven and earth. All was dark and quiet upon the earth, then God created light. He then divided the light from the darkness, creating balance and harmony. The lightness was called day, and represented that which can be seen. The darkness was called night, representing that which cannot usually be perceived.

Then God proceeded to divide the waters from the firmament, creating the earth and the heavens, dividing up the land from the waters and the seas. He created abundance upon the earth, with trees, flowers and fruits. He created the seasons of the year, also the sun, moon and the stars. He made a veritable wonderland of delight, with birds, animals, reptiles and insects of many kinds.

After creating heaven and earth, and everything on and within the earth, God then created man and woman in his own image. He gave them the garden of Eden (or perfect innocence) and the gift of free will. They had the free will to leave the state of innocence, and to eat of the Tree of Knowledge, of good and evil, to become wise in the ways of the world, and to perceive the difference between good and evil, to understand hate in order to know love, and to feel loneliness in order to appreciate fully the love of God.

Both Adam and Eve were in a euphoric state of innocence, and when Eve (or intuition) finally decided to eat fruit from the Tree of Knowledge, she was able to cajole Adam (or the logical mind) very easily. This was no accident, but part of the divine plan that led them to the gateway of the knowledge of good and evil. Like everything else the snake was also a vitally important part of the great evolutionary process. If they had walked around in a state of 'sweet innocence' for eternity, this would have brought about such an unhealthy stasis, it would have probably stopped the process of creation altogether.

During their lives Adam and Eve learnt about sadness and joy, and the difference between good and evil. They most certainly lost their innocence, but they also gained wisdom through their sorrows and the difficulties that they encountered. They needed to lose their childlike state in order to struggle and achieve a new stage of conscious awareness; the wisdom of innocence.

The serpent made a promise to Eve when she hesitated about eating an apple, the forbidden fruit, from the Tree of Knowledge. The serpent said, 'If they ate of the fruit, they would surely not die.' The serpent was very truthful indeed when he said, 'Your eyes shall be surely opened, and ye shall be like God, knowing good and evil.' Let us understand the different levels of death, for life is a continual process of death and rebirth. Adam and Eve died when their perfect innocence was withdrawn after eating the apple, they were then reborn into a different understanding of life, just as a child goes through the different stages of growing up. As we reach maturity we go through many stages of death and rebirth in order to gain knowledge, wisdom and purity once more.

The God within each one of us knows that it will not be possible for us to achieve an illuminated state of consciousness in one lifetime, and that it is not possible to understand the feelings of a man and a woman, a thief, saint, sinner or king in just one life. The God within each of us knows that we need to have many experiences in different types of bodies, before we can even begin to comprehend and feel the stirrings of the limitless compassion and love of God within the heart. In order to become divine, it is also necessary to become human.

The psychic-genetic imprint

The great wheel of rebirth started to revolve from one life into another, experiencing many wonderful things, and discovering creative, artistic and scientific gifts that were not even suspected.

Through these special gifts, we are able to resonate more deeply to different aspects of life, enabling us to become more holy. However, during this quest for wholeness, many mistakes are naturally made. Sometimes we become too proud of our achievements, other times jealous, revengeful and angry. Sometimes these emotions not only hurt us, but also others.

When these negative feelings are not expressed, they become like cancerous sores within our physical and emotional bodies. Anger burns the delicate structure of the aura (our psychic sheath shaped rather like an egg) protecting the physical body. Hate blocks the mental and emotional energies from resonating properly with the environment; as with greed, sloth, envy, bitterness, depression and despair. Whatever the negative emotion, it inhibits the wonderful, limitless essence of love. We are creative beings with great potential, the unresolved negative parts creating great burdens that weigh heavily within. Through neglecting these negative emotions, they become more deeply embedded within the mind, emotions and the body. Every unresolved emotion becomes like a fossil, creating its own psychic-genetic imprint.

The physical-genetic structure which resides within the cells of the body, imbibes the physical characteristics of both the mother and the father, as well as ancestral traits. We also carry parental and ancestral mental and emotional similarities.

As it is stated in the Bible: 'The sins of the father being visited through the generations'. Here we are referring to the physical, mental and emotional genetic patterns just related to this lifetime's experiences. Then we have the positive, as well as the negative, psychic-genetic patterns to integrate and harmonise. This is part of the great divine alchemical process. Here we are not attempting to turn lead into gold, but static, unlived energies into the pure golden essence of unconditional love.

We are on exactly the same path of destiny as Adam and Eve, for we carry within us the seeds of the psychic-genetic, as well as the physical-genetic structure. We are walking on the path which leads in the same direction, to direct knowledge of God or love. How can any of us survive without the nourishment of love? It is that special essence that propels the nucleus, creates the atomic structure, balances the spaces between the atoms, keeps the sun and moon in the sky, animates the physical body and energises the air we breathe. When this energy is amplified billions of times, in a state of meditation, or when we touch the hem of love's garment, only then do we get a little glimpse of infinity.

Resolving our complexities

Before we are able to expand our consciousness into these limitless spheres of energy, we first need to work on all of the unresolved complexities that reside within us.

It is rather like starting a very personal and special adventure when one embarks on one's own personal quest for the awareness of God. It can be an exciting as well as a perilous journey. When difficulties or danger occur, an individual can often convince him or herself that all is well when there is really a great deal that needs to be understood about a particular mental or emotional attitude, or a fixed idea.

If, for example, we have irrational fears, we need to ask why they are there. If we have feelings of strong hate about a particular individual, culture or race, this indicates that there are some unresolved experiences that need to be understood. If we find ourselves living out our mother's or father's negative attitudes, this enables us to realise that we are carrying within our psychic-genetic structure unresolved parental emotions as well as our own. This is a very common occurrence; it just needs to be recognised within ourselves. We also carry within our cells all our positive as well as our negative childhood memories from this life. We are exceedingly receptive, sensitive beings carrying within us memories that have consciously long been forgotten.

We also have within us religious and cultural conditioning, that has nothing directly to do with us. The fact that we incarnated into a specific race or religion, indicates that the individual needs to learn something special from that particular experience or belief, even if it is only to become strong enough to rise above it and to connect with one's own real identity, and not simply to follow others blindly. When someone is asked what religion they are, often they say that they are a Protestant or Catholic or whatever the case may be, because that is the religion of the person's parents and they feel that this is sufficient, instead of going on his or her own individual quest for religious experience, and spiritual truth.

Often a person is living out a parental problem as well as personal ones. An individual could even be carrying his or her father or mother's unlived shadow. A phobia could belong to a parent, for example a fear of death, people or sex, a desire for alcohol, fear of flying, fear of heights. If there is a similar weakness in the offspring, the parental problem simply amplifies the existing problem; if the memory is surrounded by unresolved emotions, it can become locked into another time zone, and the unconscious part of the self becomes absorbed by the problem. When this happens a lot of vital energy is wasted, as the person struggles to keep their negative memory submerged well below the surface of the conscious mind.

Everyone is at a different stage of development in their evolutionary process, although we all suffer from similar problems inasmuch as we all have human bodies and therefore very human emotions. However, if one, for example, had been a Tibetan monk, and did a great deal of meditation and purification, then it may not be necessary in this life to go through as much regression and purification as one who had perhaps wasted a previous life in a drunken stupor or losing precious time through

22

indulgent idleness. Everyone is so uniquely different that one really cannot speculate about the spiritual development of another individual.

Some of us have a great inner desire for change, whereas others are simply curious. Either motive is fine, but the curious often become quickly bored and are for ever seeking new sensations, easily resisting change when going through a difficult stage in their development. On the other hand, if a person has a genuine desire for change, then usually they keep their promise to themselves, remaining within their own process of inner growth.

Ways of transformation

All of the therapies we look at below have a perfect validity in their own way, depending very much on the specific needs of the person seeking the internal transformation process. Here you will discover the main links as well as differences between regression, Pre-Creation and Psycho-Regression therapy.

STRAIGHTFORWARD REGRESSION THERAPY

Regression therapy has been practised for many years, and is a straightforward regression enabling you to travel back in time to your early childhood or past life experiences, in order to experience what you were in other lives, by reliving the past memory through visualisation or hypnosis. This also applies to reliving childhood experiences connected with this life. Regression can also help an individual to work on one particular fear/phobia/obsession, or to understand the cause of one specific problem, and this may be all a person wishes to deal with. In many instances of regression one finds that people experience themselves as 'victims' more than 'aggressors'. However, the soul needs to experience everything, including being the 'aggressor' on its journey to wholeness.

Regression under hypnosis can reprogramme a person's mind, for example to stop smoking or maybe overeating, but if they do not understand why they did these things in the first place then the problem is really not solved, it is just shelved for the time being. This type of straight-forward regression, whether under hypnosis or through visualisation, does not usually release the corresponding negative emotions and psychic conditions that surround the experience, and these remain within the psyche. *This is what is called the psychic-genetic imprint.*

After regressing patients over the years, I realised and understood that this psychic-genetic imprint is the vehicle for all our karmic conditions that reside in the organs and systems within the body and aura. Every organ has a personal karmic story to reveal. To discover what it is, I gradually formulated/created the following two therapies which I am about to describe: Soul Therapy and Psycho-Regression Therapy.

PRE-CREATION (SOUL THERAPY)

The reason that this therapy is also called *Soul therapy* is because the person's consciousness is taken back in time (guided by the therapist) to before creation when they were part of the divine oneness, in order for them to be energised through the *pure essence* of their divine soul. After absorbing this energy through guided visualisation the patient is then able to see (through their spiritual eyes and with a greater awareness) their body lying on the couch. They are then able to locate the main source of their problem which gets trapped in various organs of the body or within their aura. This is the karmic psychic-genetic imprint that is carried within a person's psyche from life to life, until all of the negative energies have been resolved of the person's own volition.

With Pre-Creation therapy the person releases all the corresponding negative emotions and psychic conditions. This is done without their having to experience the cause of the problem connected with past trauma, as they would do if they were having straightforward regression therapy. Therefore, Pre-Creation (Soul therapy) enables a person to release the layers of negative energy closest to the surface which have been embedded within the physic-genetic structure covering the whole body and aura for centuries.

Releasing past negative emotions can be likened to the peeling of an onion or stones found on a geological site. One layer is released or removed and another one appears, each layer revealing another and so on until the core of the original source of the problems is cleared.

Pre-Creation enables a person to release their negative emotions without having to relive the trauma surrounding the release of these emotions. The patient may then eventually need to understand the circumstances relating to the trauma and fears, and also why these negative energies occurred, but if he or she is too fearful to contemplate being regressed, he or she may be far happier to release the fears and associated negative energies through Pre-Creation initially, before facing the origin of the fears through Psycho-Regression therapy.

PSYCHO-REGRESSION THERAPY

Psycho-Regression therapy can enable a person to transmute and to integrate that which Dr Carl Gustav

Jung called 'the Shadow' or the unintegrated part of the psyche. Many people do not realise that they have a shadow side to transform. Usually at this stage of their evolution they keep to more physical and emotional experiences, perhaps omitting inner development and therefore change (although life itself is change, so one cannot really avoid it). However, it is necessary to get to an inner state of really wanting to understand the self before conscious action can be taken.

In Psycho-Regression you are releasing all the negative conditions associated with the past memory, as well as locating the past traumatic circumstances connected with the primal cause of the condition.

During Psycho-Regression, after the person is relaxed on the couch and has strengthened their energies through visualising themselves in a beautiful place in nature and absorbing the harmonious energies around them (guided through this visualisation by the therapist), their spirit is then ready either to travel back through the years or they can visualise themselves travelling into their own body to the source of their trauma.

With Psycho-Regression the person goes into the trauma, as well as releasing the corresponding negative emotions. For example, we may have vague remembrances of a violent death connected with another lifetime, which may manifest as an irrational fear, like fear of gas, connected with being gassed, or fear of water, connected with drowning or fear of heights, connected with a past accident or death.

This is the next stage for Psycho-Regression and Pre-Creation therapy. With either therapy when the patient is at the appropriate stage *as described previously within each therapy* they are able to build up the negative emotions with the help of sacred sounds resonated through the voice of the therapist, which enable the therapy to flow more easily and freely. In this special state of awareness the patient knows exactly where the negative emotion is located within the physical or auric body. This is not a state of hoping that one knows, but of knowing that one knows.

As instructed by the therapist, when a person feels that this negative energy is at the surface, then they automatically raise the first finger of their left hand, the left-hand side being the receptive, intuitive side of the body and also closest to the heart. On seeing this the therapist is aware that the patient is ready for the negative energy to be released. Ceremonial rattles are also spontaneously used by the therapist in order to build up this negative energy. If the energy builds up too slowly, the rattles are then often used more loudly in order to help to break up the negative static energy. At other times they are used very softly in order to assist with healing and strengthening of the area.

The patient then visualises the chakra, or protective psychic skin structure (see Glossary), opening within the area of the trauma. The chakras, which cover the main centres in the body, can be likened to a beautiful flower opening up. If the blockage is not in the area covered by the chakra, then the patient visualises the psychic skin structure opening, which allows the negative energy to flow out of the area. With the help of their individual Guardian Angel, the Four Archangels and other spiritual helpers, the patient also visualises the aura opening up in order for the negative energy to flow out of the organs and out through the aura.

The angels and other deific energies are also called upon so that they can immediately release and transmute this energy. I know without a doubt that the angels are helping to do this, and the patient is able to see inwardly or to know that this is happening.

Several psychics and visionaries have watched me do this therapy and they have 'seen' the negative energies leaving the patient. This is sometimes seen as being a black or grey smoke, whereas others see the energy in specific demoniacal forms or other dirty colours. Others have also seen the angels taking away the negative energies during this sacred healing process.

Sometimes the energies are foul-smelling as they are being released. The smell disappears very quickly as these energies are transmuted by the angels. The negative smells are the exception rather than the rule, and happily I have only smelt these negative energies a few times. When this does occur it is quite an event, as it confirms to any possible sceptics that *something* is happening.

Once the negative energies have been released, then the area that has been worked on is filled with divine energy which can be any colour (all of this is directed by the therapist and the angels). Then the area is linked to a special angelic force in order to strengthen it. The chakras are rebalanced and the aura flooded with divine energy. The link is then strengthened with the person's Guardian Angel and through the patient's inner visualisation.

At the end of the session the spirit and the soul are linked back to the physical body lying on the couch, enabling him once again to feel strongly connected to the physical body. After a few minutes of readjustment, I rub the top of the patient's head in order to earth him or her even more into the physical body, thanking the divine helpers before completing the therapy.

There is no miraculous panacea for change. The truth is that you have to be willing to experience who and what you really are. There is no special medicine man, woman or magician about to wave a magic wand to 'make it all better'; we have to do it ourselves, with help from experienced analysts/therapists who have a special knowledge and a deep understanding of the 'Shadow' side of people.

Talking through your fears

It helps to talk about our fears, either with a counsellor or a psychologist. However, we really need to understand their exact cause and to release the trauma connected with the event. A person undergoing a course of therapy with a psychologist has plenty of opportunity constructively to express and discuss unresolved feelings and frustrated longings, thereby releasing some of the pent-up anger. Expressing these feelings naturally enables them to become a lot more aware of their emotional reactions to themselves and the world around them. This is a very effective method of loosening up their deeply blocked emotions, but these negative emotions still have to be released.

People who have experienced psychotherapy are usually very responsive to my specialised forms of regression therapy, since their emotions are usually very close to the surface. However, such a person is usually hypersensitive, feeling every emotion acutely as a result. They also tend to identify with 'the sins of the world', as well as over-empathising with the problems of others. In this particular state they are ripe and ready to understand inwardly the true sources of their problems, and to transmute their negative energies.

A very good example of a blockage with negativity within the psyche is to compare it with a blockage on the physical level. For example, as constipation creates a blockage on the physical level, a similar thing can occur on the psychic level, inhibiting movement, energy, ideas and harmony. Whatever the level, movement is essential.

Taking a remedy for constipation may soften and loosen the faeces, but it will not necessarily clear the bowel. However, if one takes an appropriate remedy for the condition, one that softens *and* releases, then the blockage can easily be released without discomfort. The affected person will feel so much better and lighter once they have let go of, instead of holding on to, their faeces. This is where Psycho-Regression therapy comes in with the releasing and transmuting of negative emotions.

Someone can become very demoralised if they visit a psychiatrist over a period of years and they do not see any noticeable signs of change. There are, of course, some exceptional spiritually oriented psychiatrists, who have an in-depth understanding of what constitutes the darker side of men and women's nature, with a true knowledge of their divine potential.

However, the average psychiatrist and psychotherapist helps a person to know themselves a lot better, enabling them to come to terms with problems usually encountered in this life, to understand why the person acts in the way they do, and to become aware of what is generally considered to be antisocial, difficult or mad. It is vital that the therapist does not even attempt to influence a person into conforming to a set pattern of behaviour. For example, if a person is unusual in their lifestyle, mode of dress or ideas, they are often considered to be 'eccentric' because they do not conform to what is considered to be a normal pattern of behaviour. This is why it is so essential that the therapist is very open minded in his/her approach to the person being treated. A psychiatrist or therapist could assume that a person is mentally ill simply because the patient is able to see into other dimensions of reality and talk to invisible beings which the therapist or psychiatrist personally cannot see or hear. If the therapist does not have the same clairvoyant faculties he could easily assume that the patient is talking to an illusory person.

We are not clones, but individual beings, with enormous potential and limitless creativity. We are capable of becoming whatever we want to be. If we are prepared to put the time and energy in to dream a dream, it can well become a reality.

Different dimensions

Time takes on completely different dimensions outside of the realms of the mind. We reincarnate many times over a period of thousands of years in order to understand something about unconditional love, humility, caring, patience and trust. During all of our experiences throughout the process of death and rebirth, we are given the gift of 'free will'. This basically means that we have the choice to work with the unfolding of God's will or live mainly for ourselves and personal pleasures. If our desires become very self-orientated they can develop a life of their own which one can easily identify with, imagining this to be the only valid reality. In this way it is possible for us to detach ourselves gradually from the divine source of energy.

We create an artificial reality through identifying with feelings of craving, desire, longing or selfishness, which stop us from realising our own true spiritual identity. We can even fool ourselves into believing that our mask is our true reality. It may take many incarnations for us to realise that we can change ourselves and we really have to take the responsibility of transmuting our own karma. Through our own past actions we create all of our positive and negative karma that resides within the psychic-genetic structure in every cell of our body and aura in our present life. This imprint of both negative and positive karma reveals our own personal level of spiritual maturity and wholeness.

If in a past life we have been a musical genius, a great scientist or artist, these abilities will remain within our psychic-genetic structure. This past element of genius may not be active in our present life, as another totally different type of learning experience may need to be developed in order for the psyche to become more integrated. This is why many psychics may see musical, scientific or artistic potential lying dormant within a person's aura, which may not have been developed within this particular life.

During a session of Psycho-Regression therapy, the patient's inner self knows without a doubt the source of the experience that needs to emerge at a given time. One does not only go back to past negative memories, as the experiences that surface may have been quite positive and enjoyable.

There was a woman convinced that she'd had an unhappy childhood. During regression she went back to her early years as a child, experiencing all of the pleasant memories, the long, hot summers, the picnics, the beehives in the garden, the sweet smell of freshly cut grass and the connection she felt with nature, but after the regression she was quite indignant as she did not realise that she'd had any happiness in her early years. She had in fact taken the happier experiences for granted. This was not what she expected at all, for she felt that something very much more dramatic would arise. However, her inner self thought differently, indicating that she should not see her early childhood as a total disaster. She also learnt from this experience not to take life for granted.

A young German man had great aspirations regarding his previous existences. He imagined that he had been at least

32

a caesar or someone equally important. However, his inner self knew differently and took him back to the source of his trauma, when his father caught him playing with his genitals and hit him so hard that he was knocked unconscious. His problem was connected to a deep sexual guilt that needed to be resolved, the visions of grandeur covering up his deep feelings of sexual inadequacy.

The inner self knows exactly where the source of the problem lies, and leads the person accordingly to the trauma. Sometimes a person may need to release a lot of surface emotions before attempting to experience the actual source of the pain. If, for example, a person has a 'fear of the unknown', 'fear of letting go', 'fear of failure', 'scepticism', or 'self-doubt', these surface emotions can be released through Pre-Creation therapy. The person can then get down to the cause of the problem once the initial fears have been dealt with by reliving the memory through Psycho-Regression therapy. Treating a person this way diffuses their fears, enabling them to really come to terms with the trauma, understanding it without being swamped by the emotional overlay.

A man experienced great anguish as he went back to a life several hundred years ago when he was tortured. At the time that I saw him I had not developed the Pre-Creation therapy side of my work, so I was not able to diffuse the trauma through initially releasing the emotional overlay. This unfortunate young man went through some very heavy experiences, including the emotional and physical pain of being tortured as a witch. If I was treating this man now, I would first release the emotional overlay and diffuse the pain of the top layers of his emotions, so that he would not react to the trauma associated with the experiences so intensely.

As one releases the emotions connected to the past event and understands the trauma and why it happened in the first place, then a greater awareness begins to grow, the past traumas shedding themselves like autumn leaves in preparation for a new beginning.

The old adage of 'Know thy self' is still as important today as it ever was. We need to be objectively aware of the inconsistencies within our mental and emotional makeup, and to have the courage and perception to face who we really are, without this being distorted by our own fanciful imaginings of who we would *like* to be. To find heaven, we also need to face the hell within us that may have been residing there for centuries.

2

OUR PERSONAL INFERNOS

Unresolved karma or self-created problems caused by fear

Men and women are the microcosm of the macrocosm. Everything within us reflects itself in the outer world, our attitudes revealing how we really feel about ourselves. If we happen to dislike crowds, or if we only like certain types of people, this shows that there is something within us that is unresolved or inwardly unacceptable. Often rigid attitudes or outmoded belief systems go back into a past incarnation. Sometimes an unresolved idea may exist through a number of lives if the particular attitude continues to remain unsolved. One can liken the psychic-genetic pattern to a computer; if we do not program ourselves correctly through assimilating and understanding the experiences we go through, then the exercise will be incomplete; as with the computer, the results depend on what we put into the system.

Sometimes we wonder why we have such strong likes or dislikes regarding a given situation, which in this particular lifetime may not be within our frame of reference or experience. Many parts of our past experiences or programming are locked into the wrong frequency, and this explains why we may act 'out of character' or irrationally.

Unresolved karma

In present time we are generally not aware that we are carrying around with us everything that we are. We are the sum total of our postive as well as negative past. We carry heaven within us, as well as our own personal infernos. We really need to understand as well as integrate both the positive as well as the negative aspects of our past experiences; this is called karma or the law of cause and effect. Karma is a Sanskrit word meaning our fate and destiny as determined by our actions in former existences, naturally affecting our present-day lives.

There are, however, different types of karma which have to be understood and integrated. We all have religious, sexual, monetary and group and racial karma, as well as our own personal karma. All of these different aspects come up quite naturally in the right sequence during the course of therapy. Every individual is unique, as also is the karma that surfaces.

Unexplained fears

There was a young woman who had a horror of monks dressed in long white robes with cowls. Every time she saw a monk she became very agitated. She was once out walking when she saw two monks passing by, at that moment she felt very ill and fainted. When undergoing Psycho-Regression she found that she had been tortured by monks for witchcraft during the inquisition. Not knowing this before, in the present life she became a witch again as she had not broken the unconscious habit pattern of 'the victim', continuing to have this abject horror of monks in the present life. When this was revealed and she was able to understand the nature of her problem, releasing the negative emotions connected to the event, as well as reliving and understanding her situation, this inner terror was finally resolved.

A young married woman wrote to me with a very real fear. 'I am a married woman with children. In my teens, I became involved with a very fanatical Christian religious sect. I had to leave this sect before the experience destroyed my mind. Even after leaving, I was tormented by the fear of hell.' Her question was, 'Could this be the result of too many hell-fire sermons or the result of a past life?' My answer to this was, 'Possibly this experience triggered off much more deeply buried memories connected with a past life experience. For example you may have lived during the time of the inquisition when it was possible that you were tortured and burnt as a witch. The experience in this life obviously activated your deeply buried memory, bringing it to the surface of the subconscious mind, and therefore creating your torment in this present life.'

The past can affect the present life in so many ways. Some can be subtle and others, if unresolved, can affect the inner growth of this life very strongly and the person may have to return yet again to try to solve this negative karma.

BEING IN THE WRONG BODY

I met a young man who had a very strong desire to be a woman, a feeling that had been with him for as long as he could remember. He felt that he was totally in the wrong body and that he could never be loved by anyone while he was a male, though he was not homosexual. Most of the time he was filled with a deep yearning to be a woman, and at the age of nearly 40 he decided to have a sex-change operation.

Such an operation can be quite costly as well as traumatic even for a young man, and being that much older he was advised against it and was recommended to have psychological help. However, he refused help of any kind and was determined to go through with the operation. He was quite psychic, and had dim memories of being a woman in a previous incarnation when he was very happy and loved as a woman with a family, all of this being lost in an earthquake. This happy and yet traumatic set of circumstances had occurred a number of incarnations before his present lifetime. He had not been emotionally happy since that time of being a woman, so this had convinced him that he could not possibly be happy as a man. However, he was not willing to change his state of anguish with regression therapy or with psychological help, so he changed his body to fit in with his state of mind and past karma. It would have been much more simple for him the other way round.

LIVING WITH GUILT

There was a young man who was very emotionally withdrawn and yet hardworking. He had very few friends and could not relate deeply on a personal or sexual level. His sexual relationships were very superficial and he really did not understand much about love. He found that the source of his problem occurred four or five hundred years before his present life. A number of his friends, including his girlfriend at that time, belonged to a religious sect that the authorities were trying to ban. They found out that he knew the people involved, and they forced him into revealing their names, which he did to save his own skin. All of his friends, including his girlfriend, were hanged. After that he became a recluse, living alone with his guilt, talking to no one and taking his guilt with him to the grave.

In this present lifetime he was walking around inwardly very depressed and emotionally withdrawn, but not really knowing why. After going back to that particular experience in therapy he understood the reason that lay behind the guilt and depression, and realised that this was covering a deep insecurity and fear of death. Once the situation was understood he became very much lighter and easier to be with, his personal relationships becoming deeper and a lot more meaningful.

Different types of karma

RELIGIOUS KARMA

Our religious karma varies according to how our inner self assimilates our experiences and beliefs, translating this into an inner knowledge of who we really are. This enables us to comprehend the very roots of our spiritual existence without intellectual speculation.

A young man in Belgium had a fascinating experience in regression regarding his spiritual roots. He went back to the very beginning of time when he experienced being with God. During this initial part of the regression, he experienced the ecstasy of the knowledge of God when he was an angel, not wanting to go anywhere as he was in a timeless state of ecstatic innocence, just like Adam in the Garden of Eden. God communicated to him through the great oneness of all life, telling him that he was needed to travel through to other dimensions of being in order to help less evolved forms of life. This he did not want to do as he was very happy with the way he was and did not want to go anywhere.

39

However, he had no other choice than to follow the word of God or the Divine Impulse, so he left the state of innocence or Eden, and travelled to other worlds to help souls who were beginning their evolutionary journey. He knew that it was also necessary for him to experience being in various types of bodies and in different types of worlds. As he was double-sexed, he needed to go through the human experience of being both male and female, in order to understand their strengths, weaknesses, potential and dreams. As a young man in this particular incarnation he decided to study medicine and healing, and to continue to carry out God's work within a very physical world. After this experience he realised that even angels have a great deal to learn in their particular way, and they also can be selfish, although their temptations are rather different from ours. Smilingly I recommended that he did not go around telling anyone that he was an ex-angel for his own good. People would have either thought him mad or may have been jealous of his experience.

It is often said that truth is stranger than fiction, and from the things that I have discovered as a regression therapist, I truly believe that it is. You never know to whom you may be speaking these days ... it could be to an angel or even Old Nick himself!

However, religion can be a primal cause of many complex problems residing within the psychic-gentic imprint and these have to be integrated in order to bring about internal balance and harmony. Many of us have been nuns, monks, religious ascetics or fanatics in other lives. The human soul needs to experience reincarnating into many different types of personalities and we need to be able to understand all these multi-faceted emotions and feelings, assimilating them into our whole consciousness. When we achieve this state, we then become one with all life, having no barriers with any life form.

It amazes me how some people still continue to think that all this can be achieved in one single lifetime. It would be naïve to think that one could experience all aspects of emotions, overcoming negative experiences, even in a dozen lifetimes. We cannot condition how many lives we are going to lead as some of us learn our lessons more quickly than others, depending on how much we long to become consciously close to the God within us, and how willing we are to let go of non-essentials, at the same time thoroughly enjoying our lives within the physical body in the here and now.

Monks, nuns and ascetics tend to concentrate on other worlds and dimensions, the quality existence of the after-life being their main goal. Many celibate religious people work selflessly for their community and the greater good of mankind, neglecting their own emotional and sexual needs in the process. When a person lives a number of lives as a religious, they usually have, within their psychic-genetic imprint, a long reincarnational history of deeply embedded ideas regarding sin, lust and sexuality, unconsciously creating even deeper imbalances through alienating the spiritual from the physical.

The Buddha constantly referred to the Middle Path, although we still seem to have a long way to go on this path towards wholeness, and to that blessed state of inno-cence where fixed opinions and ideas no longer exist. A great chasm seems to reside within people who cannot re-concile their spiritual and sexual drive, seeing them sepa-rately and through totally different eyes. Being inwardly programmed through past reincarnational memories, they see them as rather a menacing dilemma of unreconciled emotions that should either be firmly ignored or sup-pressed.

Whether we have been monks, nuns, wandering ascetics or have belonged to a particular religion or sect, with very rigid ideas concerning the nature of God and spirituality, we still have to find our own inner state of balance. If we happen to think that we are the Virgin Mary or Jesus Christ, the Devil or a child of Satan, all of these ideas have to be worked out of our complex inner programming. There are many Homoeopathic remedies for people who think that they are Jesus, the Virgin Mary or even a harlequin. Also for people who feel that they are possessed of two wills, fear ghosts or demons. There are many remedies listed in Boericke's *Homoeopathic Materia Medica* for these particular problems. There are more than a few people who have had these problems over the centuries, and have needed to be released from these fixed patterns of thought.

MONETARY KARMA

Monetary karma also reveals a lot about who we are. During the course of our many lifetimes, we experience being extremely wealthy and we also know poverty, with all its limitations. In some lives we may have been poor but happy, whereas in others we are rich and paranoid, imagining that everyone around us only wants our money. We seem to take quite a number of lives to learn the lessons of wealth and poverty. When we have wealth, we fear losing it, and when we are poor we often cannot imagine being able to change the situation, feeling that we deserve our lot. However, as we have seen, it is possible to change the course of karma.

People tend to get very emotional about either having or not having money, putting themselves through all sorts of unnecessary feelings of guilt and insecurity, and often making money a hard taskmaster, instead of a source of creativity and happiness. Money is energy and can give great freedom of movement and creativity, which can be constructively used or abused. A miser is emotionally sick, while someone who over-spends is almost certainly compensating for something else that is missing in their life. To have the right perspective regarding money is to really understand oneself, as well as trusting the flow of abundance. If we give then we shall surely receive.

If we learn to discriminate regarding to whom we give money, then others can also benefit from the same action. If we try to hang on to money, then we stop the natural flow of its potential to help us and others who are in genuine need. If we do not resolve our attitudes towards money in this lifetime and allow meanness or over-generosity to control us, then we simply create further infernos that have to be surmounted in yet another lifetime by reincarnating with the unresolved energy.

SEXUAL KARMA

Sexual karma affects nearly everyone, for we have all had unresolved sexual experiences connected with other lives, as well as early childhood, religious, social and family conditioning in our present life. There are many experiences that a person needs to understand regarding psychic aspects of sexual trauma. I have therefore devoted Chapter 7 to sexual regression, as this seems to be an area that concerns the majority of the human race.

GROUP KARMA

Group karma also affects us. People not only choose to work out their personal karma, their souls also choose which country or racial group to incarnate into. The American Indians say that we go through all races and cultures during the great cycle of life and rebirth. We also need to experience being black, white, yellow, red and brown in order to understand the cultural essence of Judaism, the Islamic faith, Christianity and Buddhism, to name but a few possibilities.

When we have incarnated a number of times into different major world religions, we will have then loosened our attachment to any rigid form of dogma or theology, which will inwardly enable us to become stronger through spiritual diversity. It takes a very unusual and strong individual to break away from the group karma to evolve his or her own spiritual identity. However, this can be successfully achieved when the person is no longer emotionally attached to a group, and is not afraid to stand alone and follow his or her own personal path of destiny.

Group karma can also take a completely different form. Groups of individuals who may not know one another sometimes die together in a plane crash, train accident or suchlike. A person may struggle to catch a plane and yet circumstances that appear to be beyond his control may delay him and his life may be saved as a result. If the day, hour and time of one's departure from this life is planned, then one can assume that there is a link between the people gathered for the same event, even if it happens to be for the departure from this dimension into the next! There are many subtle forms of group karma. We may have been with groups of people in past lives and because of unresolved group karma have reincarnated together in this particular lifetime. However, as an individual becomes more spiritually aware they are able to develop a spiritual antenna enabling them consciously to avoid group disasters altogether.

RACIAL KARMA

Racial karma strongly reflects the positive as well as the negative aspects of each individual in the group. The many races throughout the world have different kinds of karmic lessons to imbibe like strength, endurance, non-attachment and generosity. A person may also need to learn a particular lesson very intensely and his or her inner self may therefore choose to incarnate into a specific racial culture that is in the process of learning the same particular lesson. The person will then have the opportunity to see his or her emotional problems reflected within the racial situation, the macrocosm reflecting the microcosm. During our evolutionary journey towards wholeness we need to understand the karmic lessons attached to all races and cultures in order to become whole.

All past racial and cultural memories reside within every cell of our bodies, minds and our emotions. We also need to understand why deeply buried unresolved dreams periodically emerge from what we try to keep in the unconscious. We also need to know the reasons why we have problems with many areas of our lives in present time and why we hate or love certain individuals, appearing to be totally indifferent to others, why certain things upset us when others fill us with joy and a sense of freedom, why we are attracted to certain types of people with particular physical characteristics and why it matters at all!

Your first priority is to change yourself. The late Krishnamurti once said, 'You cannot change the world, you can only change yourself, and that in turn will change the world . . .'

Weak spots and emotional overload

Every part of the body has a karmic story to reveal, depending upon past life experiences and whether a specific part of the body was strongly affected either positively or negatively. When there are a lot of negative experiences located in a particular area, this is often referred to as a 'weak spot' since the person usually has physical problems connected with that area. There can be a number of 'weak spots' if a person was tortured, crushed or blown to pieces in a previous incarnation. The person may be suffering pain in a particular area of the body and if conventional medicine does not find a physical cause for the condition the person may be considered to be a hypochondriac or at the very least neurotic.

One woman regressed into the weakest part of her body which was her bladder. As she was regressed she inwardly knew that her experience took place in America in the early 19th century. This is how she described it in her words: 'It's light, I am outside, blue sky, fence and horses, there is a corral, people are riding horses, I am wearing cowboy boots and spurs. I am on a horse, wearing calfskin trousers and protectors and a shirt, I am a male about 20 years of age, I am whipping the horse on its hind legs, really I am showing off. There are men leaning on a gate watching me, my horse has fallen on to its side, and I have fallen off it . . . It all happened very quickly. The horse then got up and trampled on me . . . in the bladder area. I feel terrible pain, but I am not dead, they are lifting me under my arms, then I am laid on a bed in a shed. It is a very hot day, the sun is hot . . . they cannot seem to do very much for me, I am hot and not altogether there. My body seems to be puffing up . . . I feel frightened . . . they have covered it up so I cannot see the area . . . I want to go to sleep now . . . It is a shame to leave the body, I have got so much to do . . . it is too hot . . . they keep coming and looking at me. I really wanted to live longer. I was a good-looking lad and could have done a lot more things.'

After reliving this experience through Psycho-Regression and releasing the negative emotions of arrogance, stubbornness and pride, gradually her bladder became physically stronger and she became a lot more energetic and lively.

Another patient was regressed to the weakest part of her body which was the womb. The first thing she saw was herself standing on top of an unlit bonfire tightly bound to a pole in the middle. She felt herself to be a young woman and was very frightened when she realised that she was going to be burnt alive for witchcraft. She saw lots of hooded men standing around the bonfire, waiting to watch the burning. Her terror became stronger as the fire was started and the greatest fear of all gripped her at the moment of realisation, when she knew that the unborn child that she was carrying inside her was also about to die.

After this particular regression the negative emotions released from the womb were 'grief', 'anger', 'resentment', 'fear' and 'terror', as well as feelings of loss.

RELEASING EMOTIONAL OVERLOAD

If there is an emotional overloading of trauma in several parts of the body, a sensitive person may feel ill at ease without knowing the reasons why. The person may hope that pills or a holiday will somehow solve the problem. However, if these traumas are allowed to fester internally, without attempting to resolve them, then these emotions become even more deeply embedded within the psychic-genetic structure of individual organs, or even through the whole of the physical body and aura. The physical disease within an organ is the very last manifestation of the illness. When the emotional overload is released through therapy, the organs become more relaxed and energised. The person then begins to feel more life within the body and the aura, no longer having to expend unnecessary energy trying to hold down the trauma to keep it within the subconscious. The divine energy that permeates all living things is then able to flow far more easily into all of the organs and bodily systems, thereby releasing the inner hells that torment the emotions and the mind, in turn affecting the harmonious functioning of the physical body.

There are a lot more negative psychic factors involved that could be encountered with a person regressing into the organs, like unresolved karma including witchcraft, black magic, spirit possession and psychic injuries. The more esoteric aspects of some of the psychic causes of disease will be described in the following chapters.

Heaven can truly reside within us, but no one can promise us heaven or threaten us with hell flames as both are inside each one of us. The hell within us may be self-created problems caused by fear, phobia or guilt in one of its many disguises. On the other hand it may be unresolved karma which needs to be cleared.

3

UNDERSTANDING NEGATIVE KARMA

When people talk about karma they think of it as an immutable and rather formidable dark enemy that they can do little about. Karma is generally treated like an incurable disease with many people being virtually unaware that one can really clear karma or the shadow side of the self in all its myriad forms. The word karma is generally used very liberally in order to cover all unresolved past negative actions that have accumulated over many lifetimes.

Naturally everyone is at a different stage of spiritual growth and evolutionary development, so there is no general yardstick regarding how much individual karma we need to work out. If, for example, one had been a Buddhist monk meditating in the Himalaya in a recent lifetime, perhaps one would not have as much negative karma to release as would be necessary if one had wasted precious time by doing very little for oneself or others. We can only work on what we are inwardly made of; if we are selfish, greedy and uninterested in the world about us, then this is what we project.

However, we can really differentiate between the effects of positive and negative actions by experiencing many different kinds of incarnations in order to teach us the art of discrimination.

We often take centuries even to begin to feel the inner stirrings of unconditional love, humility and trust in the God-within, one life being a very short span of time for us to learn the lessons that we have been incarnated for. Even before conception we know why we are incarnating, as well as why we have chosen our particular parents. If we have chosen a difficult family background where maybe our parents get divorced, or our conception was an 'accident', then inwardly we chose these conditions possibly in order to gain strength, understanding or detachment, or perhaps we chose to come in order to help the parents we incarnated through.

There is no such thing as an accident, only conscious inner choice as a result of one's past actions in other existences. We must realise that every positive and negative action we perform in this life has repercussions; when we harm others we automatically harm ourselves, and as we are all one we cannot really stop this from happening. When we throw a pebble into a pool of clear water, ripples spread out as a result, becoming one with the pool again once harmony is re-established.

We may have within our positive psychic-genetic karmic memory bank past experiences like being a great artist, musician, philosopher, scientist or writer. During that particular existence we may have become too obsessed by that particular aspect of ourselves and neglecting other types of experiences, this particular ability not surfacing again until other parts of ourselves have been equally well developed. We may also have been a seer, healer, priest, monk, magician, high priest or sorceress and in some specific way we may have abused these powers.

The guilt concerning past actions, including abuse of spiritual and psychic powers remains within the mind, emotions and auric vestures, acting like a psychic cancer. If these energies remain ignored and therefore unresolved, they can continue to accumulate within the various levels of our being, as well as in the different subtle layers of energy within the auric fields. They can also reside within our cellular structure, affecting the physical mobility of the organs and the flow of blood. All of these unresolved, congested emotions deplete the physical vitalities, sometimes as a result manifesting 'unaccountable depression', irrational thought patterns and feelings of abject despair.

Some negative types of karma

If one is preparing to slay the dragon, it is a good thing to have at least some idea about the nature of the beast. If St George had pretended that the dragon did not exist, it would have killed him instead. One cannot be naïve about the constituents of karma, and how it affects us personally. If we ignore the implications, we could be likened to the ostrich which buries its head in the sand, imagining that nothing can harm it if it remains in that position.

Like Pandora in Greek mythology, we have to open the box of the unconscious mind in order first to reveal, and then transmute, the shadowy nature of our personal past demeanours. As Pandora we also need hope within us, as well as strength of will, integrity and truth, before embarking on our quest for wholeness. In the ancient Egyptian mystery schools, initiates who sought to purify themselves from negative karma had to undergo a minimum of 360 hours of purification, then they were put into a sarcophagus with all bodily functions being suspended for three days and nights. During this time they were taken out of their physical bodies and had to face all of their karma, including the spirits, demons, devils, black magic influences, curses and unsavory pacts, perhaps even with the devil himself, which had accumulated from previous existences. As long as the initiate had trust in God during this time he was absolutely safe, the energies being released and transmuted through the direction of God and the assistance of the angelic forces, as well as other divine helpers. If, however, he became fearful, over-identifying with the energies, he was then not able to complete the initiatory process and would have to go through it all again, possibly in the same life. However, it was more usual for the initiate to gain further inner strength in order to complete the initiatory process in another incarnation.

Within this busy modern-day world, where the majority of people are struggling to earn a reasonable living, bring up a family or simply to be happy, ideas of temples of initiation may seem like faded dreams of an age gone by. The idea of transplanting such a unique possibility into the 20th and 21st centuries is not usually contemplated. However, there are many and various religious and spiritual disciplines to enable a person to purify himself. For example Mass with Holy Communion, which enables a person to become energised and revitalised through the power of the living Christ; different healing services that enable a person to receive healing for many different types of physical, emotional and psychic conditions; American Indian sweat lodges that assist the person with purification on all levels; meditation which clears the mind enabling a person to make a divine connection, including the Sahaj Marg system of meditation that can help a person to resolve negative karma and become one with God.

Until now there has not been a comprehensive system of purification for the man-in-the-street, who does not necessarily follow any form of religious path or dogma. It is also possible to encompass this type of purificatory system within one's life while earning a living, being in a loving relationship and generally enjoying life to the full. There are no external rules to obey, one only needs to listen to the voice of the intuition and to follow the promptings of the soul.

External influences

A person usually lives numerous lives before he even becomes aware of the fact that there is a negative karma to transmute, as well as a positive karma to enhance. As previously mentioned, the negative psychic-genetic structure resides within every cell and organ of the body, building up like the layers of an onion over the centuries, the deeply-buried negative emotions attracting all kinds of psychic debris.

We can never be possessed or taken over by any kind of external influence, unless there is a corresponding weakness within us. There are many different types of spirits, demons and devils that strongly resonate to different types of weaknesses in people, as well as vibrations in places and some of these beings inhabit and live off the physical life force. There are external demons which get trapped on this earth plane, because of problems connected with their own evolutionary process. During their life here, they become attracted to corresponding weaknesses in humans, as this gives them a lot more vital energy to enable them to perpetuate their existence. There are also self-created demons and spirits, which Dr Carl Jung, being an analytical psychologist, politely called 'autonymous complexes'. These are negative energies that have built up over perhaps many incarnations, thereby attracting other psychic life-forms as a result of the person's unresolved karma. These life-forms imbibe enough negative energy in order to create and prolong their life sometimes for thousands of years, until they are finally recognised, transmuted and absorbed into the limitless oneness of all life.

One of my spiritual teachers, the late Bishop Richard Palatine, graphically described these creatures as 'the images of menace', being creatures of all shapes and sizes, and looking very much like the kind of negative emotions that they feed off. And the artists Hieronymus Bosch and Salvador Dali seem to have a very good idea of what they can look like, portraying them in amazing detail in many of their works of art. We see the traditional red or black devil, complete with horns and tail, in many Roman Catholic holy pictures, as well as portrayed in many forms in religious art throughout the world.

These creatures are manifestations of energy that have cut themselves off from the source of all life, developing their own devolutionary path of self-destruction. They are not 'happy' as we know the meaning of the word, but their attraction to the path of self-destruction is meaningful to them, as it is *their* idea of creativity. It is pointless feeling sorry for them, because they would only feed off the pity. A detached compassion is the closest path one can safely tread.

These creatures cannot continue to live within the human psyche once they are recognised and named by the person they are living off. Once this occurs and the patient inwardly 'wills' them to go away, they simply have to leave the person's body and aura, the spirit or demon having no choice in the matter.

When the person makes a direct contact with the higher self during Psycho-Regression, he receives a great deal of spiritual support and assistance. The Four Archangels are always present during the course of therapy to help transmute the negative energy. The Angel of Love, Gabriel, transmutes all the negative energies connected to this. Raphael, the Angel of Healing, heals the body and aura after the negative energies have been released. Uriel, the Angel of Truth removes all distortions connected to this, and Michael, the Warrior Angel, transmutes the spirits, demons and other adverse energies. The patient's own personal Guardian Angel and helpers are there to assist in clearing and transmuting the negative energies.

People do not usually concern themselves too much about the fate of the spirit, demon, devil or ghost which can also be trapped within the human psyche, these influences being caught up by negative emotions. At this stage they are unable to let go of the magnetic pull towards the devolutionary path of self-damnation. However, when the patient really *wills* the entity to depart, only then does it have the chance to alter its evolutionary pattern.

During the course of therapy the negative energy is broken up and brought to the surface of the organ, body or aura. The chakra or protective psychic skin structure is opened through the power of the person's inner connection with the divine oneness. The energy is then released and transmuted through the power of God and with the assistance of the angels. This can only be successfully achieved if it is done in conjunction with the person's free will. That is why this type of sacred therapy cannot be achieved through hypnosis, as spiritual participation is one of the vital ingredients for a successful outcome.

The demons, spirits and other forms of negative psychic energy have many and varied characteristics, and they feel very real indeed to the person possessed or affected by their baleful influences. If a person has a weakness for alcohol, some of the spirits that he or she attracts

55

live off the weakness of the will, as well as the etheric energy imbibed within the alcohol. This creates further feelings of craving, thereby attracting other spirits, demons and elementals feeding off energies such as self-indulgence, greed, low self-esteem or perhaps a demon of self-destruction, one negative influence preparing a breeding ground for the birth of a more insidious kind.

Reversing the process

It is essential to get to the state of recognition of what is actually happening to us before we can begin to reverse the process. This does not usually happen in one blinding flash, usually taking a number of incarnations to concentrate solely on the reversing, as well as the cleansing of one's karma. If this process of self-discovery is treated as an adventure rather than a chore, then one will, without a doubt, achieve good results very much more easily.

I smile a little when people sometimes say to me that they have only got one incarnation left, and that they will not have to return to this earth plane as they have transmuted all of their negative karma. Even if they had been absolutely correct they would at this stage in their evolution, be so full of compassion that they would quite naturally wish to return to help others to find the oneness. In Buddhism, the Bodhisattva or Enlightened One continues to incarnate until the last blade of grass is enlightened, their love for humanity being part of the great oneness of all life. When we have cleared our karma to that extent, we will then receive the same privilege of divine service as the Bodhisattva.

The Enlightened One has a deep unconditional love and reverence for all forms of life, no matter how adverse in manner or nature they may appear to be. Planet earth is a melting pot for all forms of dualism, the divine energies ever struggling to reconcile a balance within creation which lies even beyond the realms of opposites. Unless we are able to experience the mystical oneness of all life through ecstatic moments during meditation, unconditional love or some form of intense creativity, then we experience the world dualistically.

We are conditioned from an early age to live within the realms of opposites like male and female, night and day, black and white, good and evil. When I was in India with my spiritual teacher, His Holiness Shri Ram Chandra, I asked him what I thought was a rather unusual question and at the time I could not imagine what kind of answer he would be able to give me. I said, 'Master, what lies beyond light?' and he looked at me directly answering. 'A kind of greyishness'. He was telling me that there is a state beyond light, a dualism which cannot be intellectually comprehended.

Through Ram Chandra's mergence with all forms of life he was able to elevate and transform devolutionary energy that had broken off from the divine essence, thereby creating their own isolated existences. He accomplished this through transmitting divine energy directly to individuals in meditation, enabling them to release their own karma. Sometimes a spontaneous regression occurred or the person felt the negative energies being transmuted from the body or aura. Through this system of meditation the person gradually releases many different types of negative energies, which Ram Chandra referred to as 'grossness' or 'sanskaras' (impressions of past karmas) within the psyche connected to previous existences, which is the same as the psychic-genetic imprint. In 1977, I became a preceptor of the Sahaj Marg system of meditation, which basically means that the Divine Master is able to work through my physical vehicle during the course of a transmission which takes place whilst in a meditative state, enabling others to clear their sanskaras (or negative karma) through the power of His Divine Grace. There are a number of preceptors in many countries throughout the world, who through the power of the Master are able to help people to be released of negative karma.

Besides being a channel for the spiritual transmissions, I have always continued to do my own healing work and research. Ram Chandra thought it a good idea to follow both avenues of work, one complementing the other.

Many years after my visit to India, I inwardly understood that the Sahaj Marg system of meditation (meaning Natural Path) encompassed all of the work and researches that I had formulated, quite spontaneously, in a totally different way within the system of Psycho-Regression therapy. I continued to work with the abhyasi's or aspirants of the Sahaj Marg system, realising that some people were quite naturally attracted to meditation and therefore this system of purification worked for them and suited them best. However, those who were not specially drawn to meditation responded better to Psycho-Regression, whereas others like myself responded and understood the value of both methods. Ram Chandra understood exactly how my work was going and what would eventually unfold, even going to the trouble of telling me to keep notes of all my discoveries.

The Shadow

Although there is intrinsically only one life, every type of manifestation within this great lifeforce undergoes its own, unique evolutionary process. This includes all manifestations of what is generally called 'the Shadow', which comprises all our unresolved karmic past that we have allowed to germinate over the centuries through our own lack of awareness of the divine presence within us. Through misdirected thought and selfish action we magnetically attract a veritable army of different kinds of parasitic creatures, which feed off our lifeforce for as long as we continue to see them as a part of us.

Only through the process of reincarnating do we slowly learn to differentiate between the truth of who and what we really are, and the falsity of the energies which are able to project a chameleon-like quality, cunningly pretending to be part of our personalities in order to prolong their existence. The information concerning the existence of these creatures is certainly not new, they have usually been written about obtusely for scholastic minds within the musky annals of demonology, the information there bearing very little relevance as to how these creatures can mentally or emotionally affect modern man within his everyday existence.

We are still very simplistic in our ideas about people who are classified as mentally insane or criminal, but it seems to me to be glaringly obvious to look for some of the sources of imbalances within the plethora of spirits that can inhabit the shadow world within us.

SOME MANIFESTATIONS OF THE SHADOW

Students of Jung talk a lot about 'the Shadow', not clearly defining exactly what is meant by this umbrella term which appears to cover almost all known, as well as unknown, complexes. Many of the students of Jung that I have met over the years have not really been able to explain satisfactorily at least some of the more occult con-stituents of 'the Shadow', while considering themselves to be authorities on the subject (though one cannot really be 'an authority' on any specific subject as there is always something new to discover on a fairly regular basis). The term 'Shadow' is generally used by Jungians, but this has now become more widely accepted by other schools of thought, as well as by travellers on the spiritual path, as often as the word Karma is used. The traveller on the journey within at least knows that he or she has to work on the shadow in order to transcend his or her negative karma connected with the past and present-day existence. When the traveller finally realises that he or she cannot get away with anything, and becomes more aware of the fact that when hurting others, the traveller hurts him or herself even more deeply, creating further webs which must be unravelled in yet another incarnation.

There are many different types of spirits, elementals (see pages 61–67), dark angels, as well as other negative psychic influences, which are able to latch themselves on to individuals who have perhaps been involved with the black arts in previous lives, or people who have attracted malignant energies through inharmonious living in numerous incarnations. As a result of this they have not felt the need to undergo any type of spiritual purification in order to neutralise these unseen but nevertheless heavy influences that block the flow of divine energies within their present lifetime. These influences inhibit many activities within a person's life which they may put down to 'bad luck'.

It is interesting that black people are usually very much more psychically connected to what is happening on the astral or emotional level, intuitively knowing that when things are constantly going wrong in specific areas of their lives there is possibly a negative influence involved. Many times a black person has said quite spontaneously and without any hesitation that they have been cursed.

often feeling very suspicious when there appears to be an opposing force working against them, which seems to be outside the law of averages, especially when there appear to be numerous problems connected with love, money and health. There are naturally both black and white individuals who may put everything down to adverse energies. However, this is usually the exception rather than the rule in our Western civilisation, although in the East, people do not discount such possibilities, taking this aspect into consideration when they have a major problem to contend with.

There are many types of psychic influences that impede a person's everyday existence and here are some quite common examples that affect people from all walks of life, the way in which they manifest depending on the corresponding weakness in the person's character.

Spirits and entities
These are non-physical beings that have become magnetically attracted to a negative emotion. They may not necessarily have evil intentions, perhaps residing within a person's psyche because they are still very attached to the earth plane and simply do not wish to pass on to other dimensions. There are other types of spirits and entities, connected with the spirits of the deceased, who do not wish to change their environment, being attracted to perhaps grief, guilt, anger and resentment of the person that they are possessing, to name but a few possibilities.

There are mischievous spirits and entities, and others that predominantly feed off various negative corresponding emotions. The main difference between the two is that entities are beings that have not been human, but they may take on this or another form, whereas a spirit is the immaterial element of a human being, which is not connected to the human body. There are both positive as well as negative spirits and entities; like elves, fairies, gnomes, goblins and satyrs, to name a few. The negative spirits cause chaos and confusion, as well as being primal causes for all sorts of so-called irrational behaviour.

Demons

Many people still think of demons as little red or black devils with horns and nasty little sharply-pointed tails ... which in fact they can be. However, demon energy can be much more subtle than that. Demons can draw energy from several organs of the body, at the same time inhabiting those regions, or they can live in the aura or surrounding energy field encompassing the physical body. Demons are usually more 'solid' within their own reality, as opposed to the entity or spirit. Some demons most certainly do have ugly faces (in other words they can be strong enough to reveal features, as well as physical characteristics), whereas others appear to be more like dirty lumps of negative energy, this type of demon being far less individualised. Demons are rarer than entitites or spirits and usually inhabit more than one organ in the body from which to draw their energy.

Animal possession

This phenomenon is not understood or barely acknowledged in the West ... One often sees films advertised depicting werewolves, but people rarely believe that this can actually happen in reality. Dr Fraser Watts of the Medical Research Council was apparently well versed in the study of lycanthropy (transformation of a person by a werewolf) and of their possessing influence on human beings.

The orientals seem to have much more knowledge of animal possession, especially the Chinese: Simon Lau, Kung Fu and Qigong teacher and author of a number of books, is very experienced in this field, helping people to release the negative aspects of animals which block a person's energy. They can go through experiences of literally roaring like a lion, slithering like a snake on its belly across the floor or chattering like a monkey.

We have discovered with Psycho-Regression that a person can not only become possessed by animals, also by birds, insects, reptiles and even vermin, that also feed off the negative energies within a person's psyche, conditions that could have also been attracted by an extremely negative past experience. Whatever the reason, they can be released, along with other negative forms of psychic life.

Black magic and negative witchcraft links

These can also adversely affect the psyche, when one realises that it is necessary to live many incarnations in order to attain divine equilibrium and oneness with God. This means that we need to experience being all types of people. We need to understand what it is to be a man, a woman, an artist, musician, scientist, saint, sinner, whore, murderer or victim, simply continuing to go through many different types of experiences until we become more in tune with God's will, rather than with our own personal wants and desires. A diamond has to be cut many times before it reflects all its facets. Likewise we continue to incarnate until we are able to reflect our true brilliance. So to have lived numerous lives thinking that we have never practised black magic or negative forms of witchcraft would really be putting our integrity even higher than a saint's. At the very least, one needs to be open-minded about such a possibility.

Witchcraft, negatively speaking, is a direct manifestation of a calculated ritualistic procedure intended to restrict a human being in some way, or to take something which belongs to that person. If, for example, a person practised a negative form of witchcraft in another incarnation, casting spells on others, this would also harm the witch. These spells that have been cast on others, all have to be released whether it be in this lifetime, or in 20 incarnations' time. As I said earlier we really do not get away with any past misdeeds, for they have very far-reaching effects causing long-term problems for both the aggressor as well as the victim. This can manifest itself in the form of mental and emotional illness, as well as obscure nervous conditions that are generally labelled 'of psychosomatic origin' or just plain 'neurotic'. All of these past curses can also be released through Psycho-Regression, enabling a person to feel lighter and happier, and a lot more in harmony with the divine plan.

Black magic influences are the result of practising black magic in another incarnation, or being affected by black magic due to some inherent weakness within one's psychic makeup; desire for power being a classic example. It is possible to have black magic links with countries as well as people that one has known in other existences; we are meeting again this time around in order to learn the lesson that we did not learn before.

Regarding the black magic influences with other countries, this can sometimes have devastating results. I met a man who went to Egypt on holiday and he was exceptionally physically ill with an upset stomach, generally known by the Egyptians as 'Pharoah's Revenge'. After he had been ill for several days a very psychically aware travel guide asked him how he had offended the pharoahs. He did not know the answer to this question, but on returning to England he had some Psycho-Regression therapy and was able to release a strong black magic influence that he had carried around within his negative psychic-genetic pattern for thousands of years which had only been reactivated on his return visit to Egypt in this lifetime.

A woman came to see me before going to India to work with Mother Teresa of Calcutta to see if she had any past negative links with the country, as intuitively she felt that there may be. Her intuition turned out to be accurate and during therapy she released a number of negative black magic influences. When she finally visited the country she felt peaceful as well as inwardly safe and secure. She worked with Mother Teresa for a long duration, without any backlash from past lives there.

Past curses

These are also an exceptionally common occurrence, usually being on love, money, health or causing some other form of personal limitation. During therapy it is possible to find out if one has been cursed, has cursed another or cursed oneself, since one can be affected by any of these or, indeed, by all three. It is easy to forget that we are not talking about a single lifetime activity when talking about karma; we are talking about the effects of thousands of lives. Therefore, one should not get paranoid about the idea of releasing a great deal of negative energy as a result of many lifetimes of unresolved experiences.

Negative elementals

These are also not uncommon. Negative elementals are the unresolved aspects of the elements of earth, water, fire, air and wood. When these elements are not harmonious they reflect unresolved emotions and dis-ease within us. The essence of life hinges on the harmonic balance between these elements. Chinese acupuncture and Tibetan medicine are also based on the balancing and harmonising of the elements within the body.

The patient is given individually prepared herbal potions, thereby creating a harmonious balance within the bodily functions, which is an important part of the Tibetan healing process. There are also remedies within Tibetan medicine for spirit and elemental possession.

Gem remedies are also now being more widely used in the West. Gem remedies are liquified drops of crystals, gems and minerals, that are used to balance the vibrational state and subtle energies of the body, especially the spiritual, psychological and emotional levels. This in turn then balances the vibrational state of the physical body and, by stimulating the healing process, overcomes disease. As with Tibetan medicine a combination of gem remedies can be used for spirit possession and psychic interference.

Here are a few examples of the types of emotions to which different types of elementals could become attached. The probabilities within each individual are totally unique, however, and therefore are obviously too numerous to categorise.

a fire elemental   could be drawn to the energy of anger;

a water elemental   to grief, or other forms of unresolved emotion;

an earth elemental   to over-indulgence, greed, lust or perhaps laziness;

an air elemental   to resistance to life or being in a human body, fear of change or general vagueness;

a wood elemental   to stoicism, fixed ideas, notions and insecurity.

Psychic injuries

These are the remaining scars which we carry within our psychic-genetic structure, from past life traumas. These injuries can be many and extremely varied, depending on the types of lives we have led. It is of course possible that a person received healing for these injuries in other lifetimes. If there are no 'weak spots' in the body, then this may be the case, although it is not uncommon for a person to have several dozen injuries or more as a result of untimely deaths, accidents or injuries that have occurred in battles, fights or during some form of torture.

During Psycho-Regression the therapist works in conjunction with the angels in order to heal these past wounds completely. The healing of psychic injuries is really a very specialised and sacred part of the healing process and will be discussed at length in Chapter 5.

Dark angels and angels of death

We have heard of dark angels through biblical references, the most notorious angel being Lucifer who was originally an angel of light and sat at the right hand of God, and fell from grace as a result of the sin of pride.

The function of the Angel of Death is an essential part of our present evolutionary process. Most of us do not relish the thought of living to be too old, though we do not wish to attract the attention of this angel prematurely either, his interest becoming easily aroused when a person emanates feelings of self-destruction, self-dislike, lack of desire for living, self-hate or guilt, to name but a few possibilities.

A girl who had a wasting disease attracted an Angel of Death through her lack of desire for living. During the Psycho-Regression process she released many negative emotions which made her vulnerable to such an influence, also releasing

*the negative attachment to the Angel of Death. After this
experience, she started to develop a renewed enthusiasm for
life, even putting on some body weight which also made her
look a great deal better.*

Releasing vows and
past unsavoury agreements

During many lifetimes we have doubtless made numerous
vows, promises, solemn agreements, pledges and oaths, as
well as declarations. Probably even in our present lifetime
we have taken a few vows and made promises that we
have not, for one reason or another, managed to keep.
Nevertheless, the vows and promises have been made
and do not just disappear if we just happen to change
our minds about the agreement.

If we publicly, and of our own free will, make a
vow to remain with our marriage partner for life, then
we are making a deep psychic bond with that other
person. If the marriage does not work out and the
individuals go through the legal procedure of divorce
and then remarry, they are still spiritually and therefore
psychically connected to the first partner because they
have not publicly released one another from the previous
vows which they made.

This could be one of the reasons why the Roman
Catholic Church does not recognise divorce, although
they do not really explain the inner reasons behind
this ruling. One harmonious way of working with this
obvious dilemma is that if the problem between a couple
is irrevocable and a break-up or divorce is the only sane
solution, the couple then publicly go through a divorce
ceremony, thereby releasing one another from the vows

which they made in the sight of an all-compassionate and loving God. When the link is broken they can then go their seperate ways with the knowledge that they had acted with wisdom, legitimately breaking this vow in order that they are both free to remarry, without carrying within them broken as well as unresolved agreements causing a deep inner hurt that could adversely affect any successful new beginning. Unresolved marriage vows can naturally cause guilt or grief as a result of not genuinely acknowledging a great inner change that has taken place.

Several churches in the USA are realising the importance of this and are starting to perform divorce ceremonies. When one begins to understand the inner problems that unresolved vows can cause, it is vital that this is not just treated as a theory that cannot be substantiated or left in the files of orthodoxy to gather dust for another few hundred years.

Legal agreements are mutable, as they can be easily changed by consenting parties to the prior arrangement. Vows and pacts, by their very nature, penetrate very much deeper layers of our consciousness. These vows of our present-day existence should be broken with the person involved if humanly possible, although agreements, vows and pacts from other incarnations naturally have to be broken in another way.

Most people have made vows of poverty, chastity and obedience in former lives. For example, there was a young man who could not save money and it seemed to flow through his hands like water. He found that he had made a vow of poverty in a past life and this vow was imprinted on his hands, as well as within his heart. Once this vow had been released he found that he was able to spend his money more wisely.

One woman wanted to fall in love and to have a really harmonious emotional and sexual relationship. No matter how hard she tried, her relationships always seemed to go wrong. During regression she found that she had made a vow of chastity in several other incarnations, and these all had to be released before she was able to meet a man, fall in love and eventually marry.

Another woman who was unhappily married to a man who regularly beat her, still meekly continued to be a 'dutiful wife', regardless of how badly her husband treated her. When she finally went through some regression, she found out that she had made a vow of 'obedience' in other lifetimes, including one to her present life husband. She had also had a lot of early childhood conditioning to contend with in this life. When she had released all of these conditions she surprised her husband by totally changing her attitude towards their relationship. He was so taken aback that he stopped beating her and became a lot more cautious about the course of his actions.

Whatever the past vow happens to be, subtly or often not so subtly, it can affect the person in their everyday lives. These vows are usually connected to *poverty, chastity, or obedience,* or possibly a vow not to reveal some secret information from another existence.

When a person is not meant to reveal confidential information in therapy they should never be pressed to disclose it, because the information can always be passed on to their Guardian Angel, which can telepathically transmit the information to the being that it was originally meant for. When this is successfully accomplished through the person's inner will, guided by the therapist and assisted by the angels, the person quite naturally experiences a feeling of great relief at having released an indefinable heaviness.

It is not uncommon for people being regressed to have made past unsavoury agreements with the devil, the embodiment of all evils and wrongdoings. Sometimes people have been initially shocked by their personal revelations, at the same time realising that this was to do with past existences when their consciousness was entirely different. This type of diabolical agreement is usually connected with past personal desires; craving for power, control over people, personal wealth or deliberately drawing vital energy from others through some form of sexual aberration connected to black magic.

When a person has made a pact with the devil, they usually have fairly forcible personalities in their present lives, possessing some unusual magnetic energies to attract the unwary. They may not even be aware of this connection until they have started to cleanse themselves of their past karma in order to find and truly connect with the God-within.

The great news is that we are not puppets controlled by some greater force external to ourselves. We have the keys within us to clear karma and to become what we are truly meant to be, namely God incarnate within the physical body. We do not have to wait to accomplish this in yet another incarnation, nor in some other dimension, as this can be achieved while we are in the physical body in present time. We only have to give ourselves permission to embark on this spiritual journey, with the will-power to continue and the love to guide us on our way.

One needs naturally to understand something about karma before endeavouring to clear it. I have given you some idea of the energies that congest the body and auric fields. The karma connected with psychic injuries is another aspect that needs special consideration in order for you to have a fairly detailed, as well as comprehensive, understanding of what karma really is.

4

PREPARATION FOR PSYCHO-REGRESSION THERAPY

When working in depth during the sacred healing process of Psycho-Regression, there are always three main energies involved to help the patient to connect with the very deepest levels of the psyche, safely, effectively and dynamically. I call these energies 'the trinity' – God, the Patient, the Practitioner. If one does not lose sight of these three then great things can be achieved.

An energy interaction takes place long before the patient arrives on the doorstep for treatment (the term patient here being loosely applied to you or the person having therapy; the term practitioner and therapist being one and the same). The divine energies have already been set into motion the moment the person genuinely decides that they wish to change their lives. A number of unresolved problems may be causing emotional confusion, pain or anxiety, and the person decides upon a plan of action through investigating the different avenues of help that possibly may be able to assist him or her in the quest for change.

There are numerous types of therapy for the patient to choose from, and he or she may feel confused and really unsure about which way to turn for assistance. However, if the patient is really in earnest, God always seems to be at hand. The patient may go to a meeting, a lecture or hear something that will inspire him or her into getting more information. Things then seem to open up in the right way at the right time – not always in exactly the same way that the patient imagined or expects. But it happens anyway, as the inner need makes itself known in the spirit world. This need is then met on a physical level when the patient 'accidentally' come across the right contact to help him or her in his quest.

I know that most people are a lot more intuitive and psychic than they imagine. When they do not feel confident about a practitioner they may not logically be able to explain their feeling intuitively, feeling that the practitioner does not resonate with their particular inner needs. Sometimes the patient can feel this even before a physical meeting is initiated. The patient may feel that an unresolved problem within the practitioner somehow resonates to a problem within the patient and may therefore quickly change direction, looking elsewhere for the right practitioner and also avoiding his or her own problem.

The practitioner cannot, of course, be perfect, though he or she needs to be inwardly clear enough through his or her own process of transformation to act as a mirror for the patient to reflect the problems on to. For the sake of the practitioner's own growth and inner learning, he or she also needs to be able to relate to the patient on a parallel level of consciousness and be able to express warm-hearted empathy spontaneously, at the same time being aware of what is happening behind scenes within the patient's psyche.

The patient also has his or her own inner levels of assessment to experience, regarding him or herself, as well as the practitioner. The patient needs to be able to relate quite strongly to his or her own inner feelings and special needs, as well as feeling very secure in his or her own chosen method of transformation and change. It is not an easy task to look for the right practitioner, one that the patient can trust to help in his or her special voyage of discovery into the uncharted waters of the self. When God subtly guides you in the right direction, then, through this inner guidance, powers of discrimination and a good dash of inner trust, you will invariably arrive at the right portal in order to initiate your own process of inner growth and transformation.

The practitioner of Psycho-Regression

The 15th-century philosopher and physician Paracelsus knew that there was a good reason why a particular patient was attracted to visit him for treatment. He looked within himself for the answer, rectifying the imbalances which he discerned within the patient, realising that if he initially worked on himself there would be a greater inner connection and therefore response between himself and the patient. He then knew that the course of healing would have a successful outcome, as he had first corrected the imbalances from within through his own intuitive awareness before treating a person outside of himself. He knew that intrinsically we are all one within the divine scheme of things, and if it is really correct that like attracts like, then he first had to correct the imbalance within himself.

This approach could also help the modern-day practitioner to make a very much greater spiritual link with the patient, and unless that spiritual connection is internalised then the therapy could be comparatively superficial.

The patient

According to the *Oxford Dictionary* 'a patient' is one who is primarily under treatment. I personally do not particularly like this reference to another human being who is endeavouring to sort out the source of his or her problems. When this term is used, often quite mistakenly, the patient may assume that the practitioner is somehow set apart from the human condition. If the practitioner projects this type of attitude on to the patient, he or she is making a great mistake, as the patient will not then be able to relate to him or her properly in a down-to-earth and human way.

During the course of the therapeutic process there may be times when the patient hates and loves the therapist. *Transference* is a word that is commonly used in this kind of situation, the practitioner remaining compassionate but totally indifferent to these mood changes which are the patient's unconscious projections. When there is any kind of entity or spirit within the patient which needs to be released, then prior to therapy the mood changes could be that much stronger, particularly if the entity or spirit does not want to vacate what it considers to be its personal territory.

During years of practising this work, many a patient has 'got lost on the way to receiving therapy', 'felt unwell just before setting out for the therapy' or have decided that they do not really want to change; maybe they are fearful of changing the pattern of their life. Within these mood swings there is usually a possessing spirit endeavouring to save its own life by causing enough confusion prior to treatment to stop the patient from receiving help, therefore prolonging its own existence. This occurs until the patient realises that the inner games that are inwardly taking place are decidedly irrational and he or she goes on to transmute the spirit through Psycho-Regression therapy.

Overcoming preliminary problems

If the patient has a 'fear of the unknown', 'fear of unseen forces', 'fear of vulnerability' or has great difficulty in visualising, then it is possible for him or her to be treated initially through natural medicines like homoeopathy (see Boericke's *Homoeopathic Materia Medica*), Bach flower remedies or the Gurudas gem remedies, or through a combination of gem and flower remedies which balance the vibrations and subtle energies of the body, the emotional, psychological and spiritual levels, eventually leading to the balancing of the physical body.

These remedies help to loosen the barriers between the conscious and the subconscious mind. I have found these to be subtle but powerful, and very effective in initially breaking down these barriers in order to prepare a patient for treatment prior to Psycho-Regression therapy.

If you, for example, have difficulty in visualising, this strongly indicates that there may be some unresolved trauma connected with shock that may still be affecting the psyche on a deeper level, thereby preventing you from connecting with the world of dreams and visual imagery which is part of our natural birthright.

One woman could not visualise going to the bottom of a well, lake or sea which is the gate of the subconscious mind. Upon realising this she willingly took a special combination of Gurudas gem remedies and a month later was easily able to visualise and begin treatment. Her main fear was 'fear of losing control', 'fear of being dominated' and 'fear of vulnerability'.

Many years ago, before discovering the power of these remedies, I came across a male patient who simply could not visualise. We did very deep-breathing exercises for about six sessions. After that he then went into a deep regression in the early 19th century when he was blown to pieces by a bomb. The shock of the explosion had its effects within his present lifetime resulting in his being unable to remember his dreams or to visualise. After this breakthrough he had no problem being regressed.

Trusting the practitioner

If for any reason a patient feels that he or she is being judged socially or morally, it is more than probable that he or she will never return to that particular practitioner and the patient may give up therapy altogether. It has been known for a practitioner to be visibly shaken when something outside of the usual frame of reference surfaces during the therapy. During this time, when the patient is at his or her most vulnerable, he or she can be very aware of an involuntary emotional reaction from the practitioner. The patient could take this as a personal judgement on him or herself.

A woman once came to see me full of nervous agitation, even finding it difficult to speak coherently. It took her quite a

77

while before she was able to explain why she had come. With great trepidation she told me that she had stolen objects of little value. As she told me this she was visibly perspiring with fear, fixedly awaiting my response. My spontaneous reaction was that she must be feeling very lonely and unloved, and with this reaction she burst into tears, admitting that this was absolutely true. She was feeling unwanted and neglected physically and emotionally by her husband. Once she saw that there was no judgement from me, we were able to begin the process of uncovering her problems. Trust had to be created first, before any therapy could begin.

There was a man who came for advice. He sat very fearfully on the edge of his chair trying to find the words to tell me what he was feeling. He talked around his problem for a long time, then I told him directly not to waste his time or mine by not discussing what he was really there for. Then, almost in a cold sweat, he told me that he had been with a prostitute because his wife was ill and therefore not interested in sex. He looked very hard at me while he was telling me this, waiting for condemnation of his behaviour. My instantaneous reaction was that although he had got physical relief, the experience was probably not too emotionally satisfying. When he saw my reaction he then visibly relaxed and was able to go on to talk about his real feelings.

Preparation for therapy for patient and therapist

During initial contact as the patient you need to be able to give as much constructive information as possible to the practitioner who is connecting with another human being and one who is totally unique. You and the practitioner need to collaborate on the case history of your physical, mental, emotional, sexual and other conditions connected with the psyche. The relationship with your parents and how they felt about you during the gestation period is of prime importance. It is also important to find out how you initially discovered sex, as well as parental and religious ideas about sexuality, and chronic fears and phobias. Also information concerning the quality of emotional relationships throughout your life and whether they followed a recurring pattern must be discovered.

There is a great deal for the practitioner to assimilate before working out which 'bombs' initially need to be defused within the minefield of the human psyche. Often this can work out quite naturally through your own inner guidance during the course of therapy. However, the practitioner still needs this information at his or her fingertips in order to use it when it is required, for example, if there was a great emotional difficulty with the mother, father or grandparent. This information could be constructively used at the right moment by a therapist with a thorough initial understanding of the hurdles that need to be encountered during the course of therapy.

During the period of discussing his or her case history the patient gradually becomes more relaxed as their life pattern unfolds. The practitioner and the patient establish a feeling of trust, the patient needing to be able to divulge his or her innermost feelings. This total trust may not necessarily be established during the first session. However, the deep interraction regarding the patient's feelings usually goes a long way to establishing this trust if the patient and practitioner are going to work harmoniously together during the course of therapy. Although the first session mainly comprises talking, it is exceedingly intensive as the whole life of the patient is revealed in order to uncover the problem areas that need to be dealt with. The first session will set the healing process in motion.

Some patients want to understand the source of particular fears or phobias and so they may come for approximately half a dozen sessions. On the other hand, if a patient genuinely wants to clear his or her karma as much as possible in this lifetime, he or she may have therapy for about 24 sessions (approximately once a month), and then leave it for a year, and continue with therapy when the opportunity presents itself or another problem surfaces and the patient inwardly feels that it is right to do so. If people are travelling long distances they often have three or four session over four days and then leave it until they are able to return again. There is a group of women from Finland who visit England at least once a year for four or five sessions and they take the Gurudas gem remedies to work on their negative emotions during the long period when they are not having therapy.

A therapy session usually lasts from two to two-and-a-half hours, which includes discussing the problems, then having the therapy and discussing briefly what took place. The patient may feel wonderful after the session, and much lighter, sometimes the face looking as though it has shed 10 years. Or perhaps they may feel a bit dazed or emotionally detached, in which case a natural remedy can be given by the practitioner to clear up any feelings of emotional shock, for example a Bach rescue remedy or Gurudas first-aid remedy. During the next few days the patient may feel very high spirited or very low, usually at one extreme or the other, whichever way the emotional swing happens to go. Quite often it swings wildly in both directions until the emotions find their own new natural equilibrium. Sometimes a session reveals a negative emotion that may have been lying dormant, so the patient may visit the practitioner feeling anger, hatred or sadness. Whatever emotion the preceding therapy has uncovered this can be dealt with in the following session.

Commitment is important for the patient if he or she wishes successfully to work through his or her problems, otherwise the patient is wasting his or her time, as well as the practitioner's.

Notes for practitioners

Another very important area to consider prior to treatment is the patient's religious background and beliefs. If he or she happens to be an atheist but is open-minded enough to believe in the possibility of reincarnation, then it would be possible to regress the patient in order to find out why there is no connection or feeling for the divine law that governs all life (the source of infinite love), known and acknowledged by many as God. It is not uncommon for a person to have all kinds of negative emotions concerning God, but they usually keep these feelings very secret for fear of what others may think, including the practitioner. The patient may find it very difficult to admit to being an atheist or to express negative feelings concerning God.

For example, there was a woman who was tortured for her spiritual beliefs in another lifetime, and when she was about to die she felt that God had abandoned her because she had not been saved from the rack. She had carried these emotions with her into this lifetime and she felt a great deal of anger and rage against God, as well as her feelings of abandonment. When this was worked on in Psycho-Regression her attitudes changed over a period of time as she began to see life in a very much wider perspective, allowing a deeper part of herself to surface and experiencing a loving feeling towards the God she thought had abandoned her. She began to understand why that particular life as a 'victim' had been a form of self-inflicted guilt which was a result of inharmonious acts directed against others in preceding incarnations. It was difficult for her to understand that there was no angry God judging her for all her past misdemeanours and punishing her like a naughty child; she was indeed her own judge, jury and executioner.

People following particular religious doctrines should also be treated within their own frame of reference in order to feel familiar and secure within the therapeutic process. There are angels within all religions, so most people take quite naturally to the idea of working with angelic presences within the course of therapy. They usually feel very comforted by the idea of working with their own personal Guardian Angel, and spiritual helpers and guides.

If the patient happens to be a Buddhist then the Buddha will be called upon; if a Christian, Christ is called upon; if a Muslim, then Allah, if a Jew, Elohim or Jehovah. When an African or a West Indian is a Christian, but has roots in his or her own culture, I then also call upon the patient's ancestral energies to help in the quest for wholeness.

A Muslim woman came for treatment and she was not happy with the statue of the poet and philosopher Dante Alighieri in the room where the therapy was taking place. She saw it as a graven image and asked to have it removed. With reverence for her religious background this was done without a second thought. During the course of Psycho-Regression therapy, Allah was called upon by the practitioner, after which she released a number of spirits. In the Islamic

*faith these are called jinn, therefore she did not refer to
the term 'spirit' but to jinn. Within this context she felt
secure and they were then able to proceed smoothly without
any more ado.*

It is essential that the correct spiritual energy is called
upon to help the individual patient and that the practitioner does not fall into the trap of imposing his or
her own religious beliefs and background on to that of
the patient. If the therapist works with the patient's
spiritual energies then dynamic results can be achieved
for both.

It is not enough just to regress the patient back to an
early childhood trauma experienced while in the womb
or a problem connected with another incarnation. All
of the negative emotions have to be released, as well
as the negative influences associated with the trauma
in order to get a truly effective result. It is rather
like bursting a boil. One can burst it, but one must
get all of the pus out in order to clear the condition
completely, allowing it to heal. Likewise, in many cases
of straightforward regression therapy the poison is not
always truly eliminated.

The preparation prior to Psycho-Regression is of paramount importance. It is not just a case of getting the
patient into the subconscious as quickly as possible. The
therapist helps the patient, when lying on the couch, to
relax each part of the body through guided visualisation,
in order to be receptive enough to link in with the
angelic helpers, enabling the patient to feel energised and
inwardly able to understand whatever inner experience
may present itself. This is why the spiritual aspect of
the therapy is so important, as some of the experiences
encountered can be very heavy, whereas others can be
amazingly illuminating, giving a person a much greater

understanding of him or herself and the energies that can subconsciously inhibit his or her life.

Taking you (the patient) on the journey to the subconscious

When your whole body has been relaxed you then visualise yourself in natural surroundings. This could be a garden, beach, mountain scenery, desert or wood. Feeling relaxed and secure, you visualise yourself, with the help of your therapist, to be in the desired place, enjoying the peace and tranquillity as well as energising yourself with energy from the natural forces. You then walk down the garden, the beach or the wood, always walking downwards because you are walking towards deeper levels of consciousness, until you find your chosen well, lake or sea.

At this point you are made consciously aware that your Guardian Angel is there to accompany you on your journey, enabling you to feel a great deal more secure, especially if you are a little nervous of the unknown. If you have difficulty in believing in angels, then you become intuitively aware that a spirit guide is accompanying you (most people undergoing such in-depth work usually have a desire to make contact with their Guardian Angel and are more than happy to do so). You then walk, for example, to the sea with your Guardian Angel, feeling relaxed and secure. You start to walk into the sea until the healing waters cover your chest, the whole time being taken on this journey through guided visualisation. You can choose either to walk, float or swim to the bottom of the sea, still with your Guardian Angel. If you happen to be afraid of water, then you can choose to go down an empty well, or float to the bottom of a canyon.

One woman walked into the sea and was very afraid to float down, but as soon as it was suggested that her Guardian Angel could help her by holding her hand, she felt greatly reassured. As she began to go down into the sea she again panicked. It was then suggested that the angel wrap its wings around her; she then felt fine knowing that she could safely go down without any feelings of fear.

During the early stages of therapy, angelic help is invaluable and ideally should not be overlooked, taken for granted or ignored.

When you have reached the bottom of the well, lake or sea, then a connection is made with the 'keeper of the inner world', this energy manifesting itself in the form of an angel, fairy, globe of light or a mermaid, to name but a few possibilities. This contact is as important as the link made with the Guardian Angel, as this connection is another natural source of energy, enabling you to be thoroughly inwardly prepared for the journey. This initial preparation is a very important part of the therapeutic process. It is essential that you feel relaxed as well as energised through the forces of nature, as well as through sacred sounds that are produced from deep within the therapist's whole being. They are like the sound of the energies in the wind and forces of nature, the sound of the universe or the divine essence.

During this therapy you are not in hypnotic or trance state, so you can immediately become consciously aware at a moment's notice. Guided visualisation at a very deep level is the best way of describing your inner state of being, knowing on a conscious level that you are lying on a couch, at the same time feeling that your irrational self is as free as a bird to travel to deeper dimensions of being, outside of the limitations of space and time.

After you have been further energised, through sacred sounds and by the 'keeper of the inner worlds', only then are you really ready to begin the inner journey to the primal source of the problem.

This special preparation of relaxation, visualisation and being energised through the spirit of nature is the same for all types of Psycho-Regression therapy.

There are eight fascinating ways of approaching the kernel of the problem, the method employed very much depending upon the needs of the patient. One cannot intellectually assess deep primal causes or, even with the most vivid imagination, conjure up what might surface from the murky waters of your complex karmic past. All the possibilities and ramifications can be carefully considered, although at the end of the day your inner self really makes the final selection.

The dangers of experimentation

It is unwise to try to go into the depths of the subconscious without the help of a therapist. The same applies to regressing back in time, as you never know what may transpire and it could create a difficult situation to emerge from alone, even if the person happens to be an experienced meditator.

I once regressed myself into another life while in the meditative state and found I was a pilot going through the experience of my plane crashing – a very vivid and real experience. However, there were many aspects of this regression that I was unable to complete without assistance, for example finding out what I needed to learn from the experience and why I was in a 'victim' situation. I also needed to work with the angels to heal the psychic injuries connected to the event (this can only be done with a therapist). I had to be regressed again in order to complete it properly. I also needed to release the negative emotions connected to the experience. This illustrates one of the major differences between straightforward regression and Psycho-Regression therapy.

Speculating on the outcome of Psycho-Regression therapy is just a waste of time and energy, the truth regarding the cause of the problem possibly being outside of one's general range of vision and only being discovered through Psycho-Regression therapy. The following example really illustrates that it is not possible to speculate on what may occur during the process of Psycho-Regression.

A man who was not able to form a relationship with a woman in this life discovered through Psycho-Regression that in a recent incarnation he was very much in love with a girl and the preparations for the wedding had been arranged. However, only weeks before the wedding she died in an accident, and his shock and grief were tremendous. After her death he became very aware of her spirit and telepathically communicated with her. That way they were still able to be very close without physical contact. He never married in that life, remaining very faithful to her memory.

This created greater problems than he had ever imagined, for the spirit of the same girl had continued to remain attached to the energy within his psychic-genetic imprint, manifesting within his aura throughout several incarnations. This was the reason why relationships in this life did not really flourish as he was still inwardly very absorbed with a love that never came to full bloom. Once he understood this situation, he was able to release the grief as well as the emotional attachment

87

to the spirit of this woman. Once this had been achieved, he was then able to enjoy a loving and meaningful relationship with a woman in the 20th century.

Alternative approaches of Psycho-Regression therapy

The following eight approaches cover a wide range of needs and work in conjunction with, as well as dovetailing quite naturally into, one another. The therapist needs the skill to perceive which method is required with each individual session, this knowledge being acquired through training, experience of and wisdom about this process of healing.

1. Travelling back through the years to the source of the problem

This is an effective, very open-ended approach, whereby the patient can travel back through the years, to childhood in this lifetime, experiencing the situation, as well as releasing the negative emotions and psychic conditions.

2. Travelling into the womb

Many traumatic experiences can be encountered in the womb which can affect the person's mental, emotional as well as psychic development, such as the parents wanting a child of the opposite sex to the one in the womb, a fall resulting in trauma or an attempted abortion. The patient may need to relive the traumatic experience that happened during the time in the womb or during the actual birth process.

As the person travels back through the years or into the womb, they are easily able to indicate the year or the month connected to the source of trauma, through spontaneously raising the first finger of their left hand (see page 27). Sometimes when a person has gone through an exceptionally heavy experience during the birth process, they may not be able to lift the first finger of the left hand while travelling back in time, suggesting to the therapist that there is a totally different primal cause blocking the patient's initial reaction. If this is the problem then the next approach would be more helpful.

3. Pre-Conception
If there is any kind of doubt regarding the primal cause then the person goes back to when they were pure mind and pure spirit, before they were consciously conceived by their parents. When the patient is in this state of clarity, they really know exactly why they chose this particular life, as well as why they chose their parents. This is a particularly beneficial stage of consciousness to be in, because if at this point the therapist asks the patient if the source of his or her problem lies in another incarnation or, in the life they are about to incarnate into, they will really know the answer without any doubt. The stage of pre-conception is like a crossroads and the patient can choose with confidence which path to follow, and he or she may realise that the source of the problem resides within the experiences of another lifetime.

4. Travelling into other lifetimes
The patient regresses to the source of the trauma in other lifetimes, and there could be a number of lives associated with the same problem. If one particular emotion needs to be sorted out, like 'grief' or 'anger', there may be several lives involved that need to be worked on. If the therapist believes that we can only experience lives on this earth plane, then the patient could unwittingly have

a problem on his or her hands, especially if he or she spontaneously regresses beyond the boundaries of planet earth. The patient's unfoldment could be greatly inhibited by the therapist's lack of understanding and knowledge of 'inner space', and other dimensions.

5. Psycho-Regression into other dimensions

There are many cases of individuals who have regressed into lives on other planets and to experiences encountered between lives. The body and the circumstances are very different from life as it is known and understood on the human level. When this occurs the therapist should not condition the patient during therapy into thinking that he or she has arms or legs. The patient's body could be a floating transparent mass or he or she might have a body that is green, yellow or red, even possessing a tail or webbed feet. When a person is in this altered state of consciousness, these kinds of experiences are not exceptional, therefore the person is not repulsed by them.

We have lessons to learn from our past experiences in other dimensions as well as in this earthly life. For example, when a person has a problem accepting or living in the physical body, this may be the result of lives lived in other dimensions when his or her body was differently constructed. Going back to this past state of being through Psycho-Regression therapy could help the person to have more acceptance and understanding of his or her feelings in present time.

The following three approaches to Psycho-Regression do not follow this particular sequence of natural possibilities.

6. Psycho-Regression into sexual trauma

A person needs to understand this life's sexual problems, including sexual trauma in childhood and experiences while in the womb. They also need to understand the source of any sexual trauma which may have occurred in other lifetimes, which can be the cause of the present-time problem.

In sexual regression the person goes back to a number of lives associated with sexual trauma, also releasing emotions and psychic conditions connected with the unresolved experiences.

In Chapter 7 we look in detail at this aspect of Psycho-Regression.

7. Psycho-Regression into the body

Instead of regressing the patient back in time, as with the preceding examples, it is possible to travel into the body to the weakest area in order to understand the primal cause of the problem.

When a person is physically ill there is always more than one primal cause. This process just has to be continued until all of the 'weak spots' are gradually strengthened.

Regressing into the body occurs when the person stands at the bottom of the well, lake or sea, after the initial phase of relaxation and prior to commencing the actual regression. The 'keeper of the inner worlds' opens the bottom of the well, lake or sea, enabling the patient to embark on the journey into the body, travelling through the top of the head to the weakest area.

This way of regressing is very effective when a person wishes to release past trauma within the organs which are causing the physical discomfort, like difficulty in breathing, heart trouble or maybe a bladder problem. In Chapter 2 you will find an example of regression into the liver and another into the womb, which illustrates this more clearly.

8. Psycho-Regression into sub-personalities

Many people are particularly interested in understanding how personalities connected with previous lifetimes affect their present-day circumstances, often having a real wish to understand all of the positive as well as the negative aspects of the personality that are not properly integrated within the psyche. This can be achieved when the person has really understood the purpose of the existence of a sub-personality, releasing the negative characteristics and integrating the positive attributes. And these personalities may not necessarily be connected with lives on this planet.

There is an amazing potential with this approach to Psycho-Regression, as individuals are able to recall, as well as bring back, knowledge connected with experiences which may have happened many thousands of years before.

The self-healing process

The wonderful thing about this system of Psycho-Regression therapy is that the patient really heals him or herself through systematically and carefully guided visualisation, and with the help of the angels, guides and other divine forces.

At this initial stage we have given you an introduction to the mechanics behind a procedure which can be extremely powerful and effective, as well as being a very natural event when it is taking place. Explaining to someone how to swim is of course very different from actually doing it, as also is Psycho-Regression each time it takes place. Therefore one can only give some examples (as I have done) of the possibilities that could occur during this very unique experience. One does not drive a car in one gear only, there being four or five gears to enable the car to run smoothly. In Psycho-Regression there are eight possible gears that can be engaged in order to achieve the desired results.

5

THE HEALING OF PSYCHIC INJURIES

We often hear about people who are broken-hearted, heartless, gutless, brainless, or people who are blind in their attitudes towards life! This obviously does not mean that they have a broken heart physically, and if they were truly heartless they would be dead. The truth is that these descriptions succinctly reflect an inner truth that is not usually consciously perceived.

People are not generally aware that psychic injuries exist, although they feel their effects within areas of physical weakness in the body, or subtly inhibiting the function of the five senses: hearing, sight, smell, taste and touch. The well-known author Dr Arthur Guirdham has made several references to psychic injuries in his books, especially in *The Psychic Dimensions of Mental Health*, but he makes no mention of how to cure them. Contained within this chapter is the first detailed information on curing psychic injuries that has ever been written, to my knowledge.

People are not consciously aware that such injuries do exist. They usually put it all down to 'Just my imagination'. In the West we never say 'It is just my intellect', the imagination being usually treated as an inferior process.

When a person has an inner fear or phobia connected with a specific part of the body, this can indicate that the person may have suffered injury in that area in a past life. For example, an exaggerated *fear of blindness* may indicate that a person has experienced such a trauma in another life, retaining deeply buried memories of this experience in the subconscious, as well as within his or her eyes. Difficulty in visualising or not wanting to see what is happening within oneself may also be symptomatic of this past experience.

Various irrational fears usually indicate that there is something that has to be understood. *Fear of going mad* may be the result of intense stress experienced in the present incarnation, or it may be covering up experiences from other lifetimes where madness did occur. A person who is not able to show any feelings or communicate love, could have a psychic heart problem, manifesting itself as a break, crack or a *hardness of heart* created by the heart hanging on to too many unresolved emotional problems such as grief, hate, envy or greed. If someone finds it difficult to walk they may have a psychic injury in their feet such as burns, or perhaps their feet might have been bound in a Chinese incarnation, subtly affecting their present life mobility.

There are numerous possibilities which a person is able to locate through Psycho-Regression. They can find out when and why the trauma happened, and locate the different types of injuries in a specific area, as well as releasing the emotions that attracted such injuries in the first place.

Every situation tells a story, and one needs to locate the source of the trauma, relive it as well as understand the emotional or psychic causes that attracted the injury at the time. Most of us have a whole karmic history of psychic injuries, this being an important part of the karmic process that needs to be healed and rebalanced. In some past lives we have suffered many different types of injuries. If the past injuries are connected to extremely traumatic emotional pain they seem to leave their mark within the psyche.

A number of spiritual healers have an awareness of these injuries and are able consciously to work on them with the assistance of their spirit guides and helpers. Many of the psychic surgeons in the Philippines, for example, are able to materialise objects like a needle, blade, bullet or a metal instrument connected to the original source of the injury, though not always consciously realising the reasons for these particular types of materialisations during the course of their operations.

Examples of psychic injuries and how they can occur

Every kind of injury that you can think of occurs within the psychic-genetic imprint. There are so many different types of experiences that we go through in previous incarnations which are strongly linked with traumatic circumstances. We would be bordering on hypochondria if we imagined that we had all of the different types of injuries indicated in this chapter. This will, however, give you a clear idea of the spectrum of injuries that I have encountered over 20 years as a therapist. There is a lot of authenticated information concerning the different types of injuries, as well as details regarding their symptomatic manifestation.

The following are some of the psychic injuries that have been worked on during Psycho-Regression therapy. This list covers most of the *negative* forms of injuries that could occur in previous lifetimes, or in the present life. However, not everyone carries these psychic injuries; they may have been healed in a previous existence through another form of spiritual purification. Some incarnations can be happy and positive, and uneventful in this particular way.

Arrow wounds   These wounds may have occurred in any part of the body, and one may feel odd psychosomatic pains in the physical body.

Animal injuries   Claw marks, bites, the body being eaten by animals, strong phobias regarding a specific animal, insect, bird or reptile.

Axe wounds   These could affect any part of the body and may be another psychosomatic symptom.

Abortion/miscarriage   This may manifest as general weakness within the reproductive organs.

Bodily destruction   Where the body has been blown up as a result of a bomb or explosion of any sort. Usually this results in being unable to visualise or connect deeply with the source of one's real feelings.

Burns   These can take place in any part of the body, causing the area to be hypersensitive or more prone to infection.

Beatings   These can occur anywhere, causing the area to be unduly sensitive. The person is often very much on the defensive, without having any conscious reason for this attitude.

Bullet wounds   Affecting any part of the body, with sporadic pains that manifest for no apparent reason. Often results in a severe weakness in the specific physical area of the body.

Brand marks   Connected with Satanic agreements. These brands have to be released within the therapeutic process

97

in order to free the individual from this time of enslavement. When a person has a brand mark they are usually controlled without necessarily realising that this is the case.

Blood   This can be blood which has been drunk during black magic rites. Again this is part of 'an agreement' that has to be neutralised in order for the person to become free. It can also be blood received through transfusion. There is usually an inner link between the donor and the receiver, and can be given as a positive balancing of a karmic debt. The blood can be cleansed by the angels of any impurities during Psycho-Regression therapy.

Cuts   Can affect any part of the body, causing sporadic pains, or feelings of general weakness.

Crushed organs   This can result in strong feelings of physical debility and some general imbalance with the organ within the present life. The symptoms may not be physically chronic, but can be irritating enough to cause general problems. This is usually a 'weak spot' for a lot of emotional trauma as well as psychic problems.

Cracks   These can occur in any part of the body, causing general weakness in the area, as well as feelings of vulnerability. When a person has a psychic crack in the heart they are often overly emotional about themselves in relationship to the world around them, tending to take things personally without due cause.

Degutting   This takes place in the intestines. There are a number of people who have been tortured in past lives, including being degutted. This naturally causes weakness within the digestive and alimentary system. Emotionally such people are usually hypersensitive as well as restless.

Difficulty breathing Either through being smothered, drowned, gassed, gagged, buried alive or possibly through a difficult labour experienced perhaps in this incarnation. Such a person is usually a shallow breather and never seems to be able to get enough air. They are usually over-anxious and tense.

Embalming If a person was embalmed in another incarnation, as for example in ancient Egypt when the embalmed organs were separated from the physical body, this can cause feelings of detachment within the present-day organ or even within the whole body. This topic will be dealt with in detail in Chapter 6.

Earthquakes There could be many different types of injuries experienced as a result of this trauma. Emotionally, 'shock' would be an important priority.

Extraterrestrial injuries/implants People are not normally aware that these types of injuries exist. However, they have been coming up on a regular basis, and research has been carried out into cases in the USA, South America and also in England. These injuries may result in obscure nervous conditions, hyperactivity or feelings of lack of energy.

Fractures These can occur in bones, causing general weakness. A fracture can occur where there are usually a number of unresolved emotions in that particular part of the body.

Fingernails When they are torn off as a result of torture, this can manifest as hypersensitivity or general weakness in the fingers.

Gouge The eyes may have been gouged out as a result of torture in a past existence. This can cause lack of awareness, even if the eyes are considered to be normal in this particular lifetime. Emotionally the blindness may be a way of avoiding the truth of a situation. Symptoms can manifest as oversensitivity of the eyes, problems of visualisation, lack of eye contact and difficulty in projecting love through the eyes.

Guillotine   The symptoms manifest as a feeling of being disconnected to the body, or 'spaced-out' sensations. Other symptoms can manifest as feelings of vulnerability round the neck, throat or head area, and when a person constantly wears a scarf or a hat this can indicate that they are feeling excessively vulnerable, without always understanding the conscious reasons for it.

Knife   This can manifest as general weakness, debility in the area or obscure pains and fears.

Loss of bodily parts   There are many varying circumstances in which this can take place. The loss of bodily parts could include the head, ears, arms, legs or genitals. Symptoms again cover feelings of general weakness within the physical area of the present body. There could also be problems with the harmonious functioning of the area.

Magical injuries   This includes all forms of black magic and negative witchcraft. The injuries can include holes, rips or tears in the aura, to the placing of objects deliberately meant to inhibit the harmonious functioning and happiness of another human being. The angels are however, quite willing and able to repair such conditions when working in conjunction with the sufferer's free will.

Martyr wounds   Religious overidentification with the pains and sorrows of a deity, saint or religious person, like the stigmata marks. This can manifest as hysterical hypersensitivity through over-identifying with 'the sins of the world'. For example, people have been known to identify with the sufferings of Christ through manifesting crowns of thorns in their heart chakras, or scratch marks over the body through wearing a special garment in a past religious life (like a hair shirt) to promote self-mortification and suffering.

Mutilation   The symptoms are similar to those of the *crushed organs*, usually manifesting as chronic symptoms, and are usually a weak spot for other emotional and psychic symptoms.

Needles   These may have been placed in the body by torture, or may be used to trap energies when used with a voodoo doll. However, this can only occur if the individual has a corresponding weakness in his makeup that makes him particularly vulnerable. This is why the process of purification is so essential.

Organ removal   This includes all internal organs, especially heart, brain, eyes, liver and kidneys. If an organ has been removed in another incarnation there is usually a weakness within the etheric structure of that organ. If it is a major organ like the heart, for example, there can be problems connected to the showing of feelings and a curious detachment in a form of heartlessness revealing itself as a result of the loss. This symptomatic picture has emerged so many times during the years of work and research that it cannot be ignored.

Pokers   Again this can affect any area of the body creating harmful burn marks, causing general feelings of discomfort, as well as emotional feelings of being violated or misused.

Poison/Potions Either usually affects the psychic condition of the blood which has to be healed and energised through angelic energies. If someone has a 'psychic poison' within their physical body, this may manifest as sloth, laziness, sluggishness or apathy, thereby attracting toxicity within the physical blood.

Potions that have been taken, for example the drinking of blood during past black magic rites, have to be neutralised by the angelic forces in order for the person to become free from the negative energies.

Strangulation The injury from this manifests itself as a highly sensitive neck or throat. Psychically the injury can look rather like a dirty brown or black mark around the throat, sometimes manifesting emotionally as a fear of expression or verbally revealing one's true thoughts regarding a particular situation.

Sexual injuries These are injuries that affect the sexual organs and reproductive system, and cause various forms of physical and emotional malfunction within the sexual sphere. Physical symptoms reveal themselves within many forms of sexual imbalances, bringing about sexual craving or possibly total lack of desire or even abhorrence of sex. The injuries can be caused by shock, torture or black magic, and these are a few areas of possibility that will be discussed in greater depth later.

Skin There can be many psychic skin conditions from the pox, bubonic plague, leprosy, burns, brands, needles and residues of diseases from past existences and conditions passed on from one's ancestral heritage, even in this present life. Reference is also made in the Bible to the transference of the sins of the father . . . so this is not new information but merely needs reappraisal. Symptoms may include irritation, skin allergy, feelings of uneasiness and dirtiness.

Thorns Can affect any part of the body, causing unpleasant pains and general psychosomatic symptoms. If a psychic thorn still remains within a person's skin or body, this causes general feelings of discomfort. Often the psychic counterpart of the physical object remains within the body and this can be released through the use of Psycho-Regression or through an aware psychic surgeon with a knowledge of injuries connected with past existences. However, there is little point in removing the thorn or object without releasing the corresponding emotions connected to the trauma.

Torture There are many forms of torture affecting all parts of the body that are too numerous to mention. The individual areas of torture need to be healed as well as the shock, trauma, physical and psychic pain connected to the event. It is also necessary for the person to really understand why it all happened in the first place. It is essential to heal the causes of these injuries and to understand the whole situation in order to let go of it completely.

Transplants When a person receives an organ from a donor (see also *Blood*), there is usually a strong past connection between the donor and receiver which is one very meaningful way of resolving a karmic debt that may not have been envisaged by the donor!

One man left his 'whole body to science' after his death, and one must reflect on the kind of karma he was trying to work out by doing this.

Trephination This is an unusual psychic injury that does not often reveal itself in Psycho-Regression.

Trephination is an operation whereby a piece of bone is removed from the skull. Many centuries ago this was done as a means of exorcism, in order to release spirits and demons from the brain. It was also carried out in Inca times for ritualistic purposes, as well as to relieve physical symptoms. In more modern times it was done in order to release physical pressure from the brain, for example that caused by subdural haemorrhage or haemotoma. A survivor of this operation is Rosa Clarke, who went through this operation in 1948 and, amazingly, is still alive and very active now at 74 years of age.

During Psycho-Regression therapy the angels are able to heal the psychic holes in the head after finding out the reasons why this operation took place and the negative emotions that were released.

Tongue (usually cut out) This often occurred in a past life when someone was not prepared to reveal important information. The angels were able during therapy to reconnect the tongue after releasing the negative emotions and finding out why the person put him or herself in the role of the 'victim' in the first place! This is not an uncommon psychic injury, and the obvious present-day symptom for this is *fear of communication and speaking the truth*.

Wear-and-tear injuries These take place as part of the general hazards of everyday life. These injuries are usually connected to some of the very human problems of ageing. There are also unusual situations connected with national group karma, for example during wartime or after major group catastrophies individuals receive angelic healing of their psychic injuries between lives, giving them time to rebuild their strength, assimilating all past experiences before deciding the main area of learning for the next incarnation.

Inter-life healing

Special types of psychic injuries are healed in the inter-life (see Glossary). I have had several interesting experiences of this.

I knew an old woman in her 70s who had had a pretty difficult life, her face was very lined and she had a curvature of the spine. About four months after her death I saw her through my inner eye in a very much better condition, with her face looking softer and less lined, and her spine having straightened a little. I saw her again about six months later and her back was just about straight. She looked youthful and very much happier as joy had returned to her eyes. The psychic healers in the inter-life had done a fine job on her, and she had obviously responded well.

Another woman who also had a difficult life emotionally was full of jealousy and resentment. After she left this earthly plane I saw her in a vision and her whole body was mouldy green, but several months later I saw her again and she had returned to her normal colour through understanding and healing of her negative state.

I met a young woman who became interested in this type of healing work and she really wanted to be a therapist, but at that time she found out that she had a massive brain tumour. She was very disturbed about this as she did not wish to leave her body, but wanted to spend her life helping others. She was not able to do this, so she decided to give her strength and support to the work, but on another dimension.

Since leaving her body and receiving healing in the inter-life, she now feels much lighter and more able to help people on this earth plane, not in the way she had originally envisaged but in a new dimension.

She has decided to be a spirit guide for a time before returning to continue with her own personal lessons on this earth.

The function of angels in the healing process

Some people really *know* that angels exist, whereas others just suspect it. In fact, we are surrounded by these marvellous and helpful non-physical beings, who are with us at every moment.

There is a whole complex angelic hierarchy of many different types of angels with very specific functions. The four archangels or 'bosses' of the hierarchy work with different kinds of energies: Raphael is the angel of healing; Michael is the warrior angel; Uriel is the angel of truth; and Gabriel is the angel of love.

A German clairvoyant, who watched a Psycho-Regression session, saw the Four Archangels around the therapy couch. The patient's main Guardian Angel was standing close by, together with the therapist's own Guardian Angel, and the special power connections that help throughout the therapeutic process. The psychic saw the negative energies accumulating on the surface of the affected area. The therapist used sacred sounds and rattles to enable the negative energies to break up and come to the surface of the organ. After the negative energy had surfaced, the psychic saw the corresponding chakra and the aura, opening and the negative energy streamed out of the body like murky black cloud.

This energy could be a formless mass of negativity comprised of many different dirty colours. The patient does not want this energy, neither does the therapist nor the room where the therapy is taking place, so here the angels congregate in order to take away the energy and to transmute it – this could be likened to a 'divine recycling process'. Some patients literally *feel* the negative energies leaving the body, whereas others just *know* that it is happening. Either way it does not matter as long as it happens.

The Four Archangels preside over the therapy with other angels assisting in different ways, according to their abilities and functions. Archangel Gabriel transmutes all negative energies connected with love. Archangel Michael, the warrior angel, transmutes all the negative influences connected with spirits, elementals, past connections with black magic, witchcraft or any other energies connected with demonic influences. Archangel Raphael assists during the healing process, particularly connected to psychic injuries. And Archangel Uriel, seemingly the most unpopular angel of all as he is the angel of truth, transmutes all distortions connected with truth including lies, misuse of power and energies connected with various forms of self-deception. At the same time, the patient's own Guardian Angel protects the body and aura while the negative energies are being taken away by the archangels.

If a person is a Christian then the Christ energy is invoked as the perfect blender of the energies being released and transmuted, and if the patient is a Buddhist then the Buddha acts as the pivot for the energies. This applies to all energies contained within the religous beliefs within the patient, with Allah, Vishnu and Jehovah being treated with equal respect and veneration, according to the individual needs of the patient.

There are also other powerful beings that work with individual therapists for specific purposes in order to achieve the optimum results. If, for example, the patient had some very heavy demonic influences to be released then direct links with Shinto, American Indian and Islamic energies, as well as other sources of power, could effectively be called upon, especially if the demonic influences were connected to the sources of these energies, the results working homoeopathically.

There are sometimes diabolical influences that really try to stop the patient from receiving therapy. One Belgian psychic saw two little black devils trying to prevent the person from going down into the subconscious, but the moment the Four Archangels were invoked they were frozen until the therapy had been completed. Then at the end they were taken away and transmuted by 'the Big Four'.

One very psychic woman saw the angels taking away her negative influences in large bags or white cloths. She didn't like spiders and found that she had one to release during the course of therapy, so the angels, realising her fear, put it in a large white cloth before taking it away to be recycled.

Most people who come for the therapy have an inner knowing that angels do exist, therefore working with the angels in therapy is not a problem for them, and even when people are sceptical they still reveal an inner trust when they are in a receptive, altered state of consciousness.

It is obviously their logical mind that causes them the problem and not the inner knowing. Some people do not think about angels in their everyday existence, although they are surrounded by literature about them and see them depicted in works of art throughout the world, on stained glass windows, in spiritual literature and referred to in the Bible, so the information is there if they wish to learn more about them.

Angels can take many forms. They can look like a human figure with or without wings, a globe of light or a spiral of energy. They usually have a predominant colour, though this appears to change according to the individual's need. The wonderful discovery that was made during the evolution of Psycho-Regression therapy is that there can be a number of angels looking after different parts of the body. They seem to reside within areas of major importance, with some people having more angels than others within the body and aura itself. It is hard to ascertain as to whether or not this is part of a karmic bonus system! What is certain is that when a person has angels in many of their organs, they seem to possess a lot more physical energy.

I feel that everyone has the divine right to have many smaller angels to help to energise the body itself, but due to past indiscretions connected with negative attitudes, a person can temporarily relinquish this right. I know that angels do not vacate their job of protecting and energising an organ if a person acts unwisely, but they can get pushed out if a person keeps thinking that he or she knows better. This usually occurs when an organ has accumulated a lot of negative memories, in other words it is a 'karmic disaster area' which needs plenty of healing and attention.

If the person has performed some very positive actions, regardless of the negative accumulation of energy, sometimes an angel will stay within the confines of the area in order to keep the organ at least operational. Often the angel is prepared to continue to energise the organ until the person is inwardly ready for change. This may take centuries if the person is not willing to change. An inner realisation may occur that could change a person's attitude towards him or herself and life in the twinkling of an eye. Angels are extremely relieved and happy when the changes do occur, since they do not have to work so hard and are able to enjoy the smoother functioning of the organ, as well as being able to help it to function at a very much higher frequency.

The function of cherubs in the healing process

Cherubs or baby angels, usually strongly manifesting joy and love, are also able to help the angels to do this very specialised and exacting work. They are usually given smaller organs to look after, before going on to look after some of the more complex areas. Each person is so unique that one dare not generalise. It has been known for cherubs to look after the ears, in order to help create lightness and joy when a person is feeling down or depressed. They sometimes look after the feet, helping the person to walk in the right direction through life. They may look after the hands to help right action, and very occasionally they may look after a major organ, but when this happens it is usually done in conjunction with other cherubs or angels. The Guardian Angel looks after the whole body and aura, acting as the conductor of the other angels present within the person's psyche. I was also very happy to learn that angels have offsprings. Androgynous, as well as male and female angels, all have different types of functions to help us on our journey towards wholeness.

One woman went to hear the Evangelist Billy Graham and she saw many little cherubs playing by the platform from where he was speaking. She was very happy to see such a delightful occurrence, as they were probably there to help to engender joy and love within the people present.

Free will and dualism

All the different types of positive angelic beings have to follow the golden rule of never interfering with a person's free will, including not altering their negative psychic-genetic imprint without the person's own will to change. The angels are able to look after an organ, but they are not able to change its psychic condition. It may sometimes be very hard for them to remain detached when they know that a person is suffering as a result of unresolved past karma, thus creating even further problems within their present life. The angels of light could be thought to be working for the opposition if they interfered, as only the angels of darkness ever attempt to alter a person's free will.

Dualism in terms of male and female, night and day, good and evil, is also reflected within the non-physical planes of existence at this present stage of our evolution, since every life-form is going through its own unique process of unfolding. Even devolutionary forms of energy will eventually change during the great process of transformation. This means that even the most satanic type of being will eventually alter its form. There is no life without change, static conditions having no choice but to change their form. When people refuse to change they become like zombies, or the living dead, and begin to destroy themselves and those around them.

Demonic energies become imprisoned by the lack of movement within different life-forms, hence they forget the original source of their beginnings. Only through change can the divine energy be reawakened within the grossest of energies. The demon, spirit or dark angelic forces that can inhabit the shadow side of life do not want to change their form, since they identify completely with

111

their negativity and are very cunning in the way that they can impress a person to believe that even the most irrational behaviour is somehow justifiable. These type of forces get trapped within the artificial reality of their own existence often for billions of years, before a person comes to the realisation that they wish to transmute their negative karma. Only then do these baleful influences have the unique opportunity to discover a new divine identity. This can only happen when the doors of change are allowed to open.

Conflicts do not just occur in countries, but also inside each one of us. In our everyday existence it is all too easy to get lulled into a false sense of complacency and we may not accept that we need to change ourselves. Change being a continuous process throughout our lives, even a dogmatic thought becomes like a fossil that obstructs our spiritual unfoldment. Change means letting go of things that have helped us to feel safe in a peculiar way, for example 'the devil you know is better than the devil you don't know'. If there is a deep initial 'resistance to treatment', 'resistance to change' or 'fear of change' then this can be altered through Psycho-Regression therapy as well as through the power of prayer and personal self-awareness generated by a person's genuine desire to know the truth.

Healing past wounds and injuries

Now that we understand how past life injuries can affect us, both psychologically and emotionally at the present time, and that the angels can help during this dynamic healing process, we will be in a much better state of mind to comprehend how these psychic injuries can effectively be healed.

A patient wanted to release some of the major sources of trauma in her body, so she went through the relaxation process and with her Guardian Angel, and in her subconscious state, she travelled to the bottom of the sea. After feeling very confident and secure, the bottom of the sea was opened and then she started to float into her own body through the top of her head. The therapist counted from five to zero and she was at the main source of trauma in her body – the solar plexus.

First, she went back several hundred years to a time when she was a seaman's wife. She used to sit at the window each day waiting for her husband to return, but he never came as he had been drowned at sea. She did not grieve but suppressed all her inner feelings of 'loss, grief and resentment' that he had died and a deep 'anger with God', whom she felt had allowed this to happen. The outcome was that no one knew how she really felt, least of all herself.

Secondly, she experienced another trauma in the solar plexus when she was a young soldier killed in battle by a sword being plunged into the solar plexus area of the body. So, during the last moments of that life she suffered feelings of resentment and anger at dying so young, and full of grief and loss.

Thirdly, during her early childhood within this present life, she experienced great 'emotional shock' at the age of four when her mother was killed in a car accident. She was also involved in the accident, severely bruising the solar plexus area therefore experiencing further 'emotional shock'.

Naturally, these are not the only experiences that affected this one area in her body, though this will give you some idea of how a negative karmic build-up can occur in a single area.

The accumulation of the negative energies from these three experiences were drawn to the surface of the solar plexus through Psycho-Regression, with the use of sacred sounds, rattles and with the help of the 'Big Four'. The accumulated negative emotions of 'grief, feelings of loss, resentment and anger' as well as the 'emotional shock' and 'suppressed grief' from this life were broken up and came to the surface of the solar plexus. These negative emotions were described by the patient as dirty black and grey energy. Once at the surface the patient is able to visualise, as well as know inwardly, without a shadow of a doubt, that the solar plexus chakra, as well as the aura, has opened up in order to release the accumulated emotions.

The angels helped to draw this dirty energy out of the body and aura, and instantaneously transmuted the energies. Then, once the negative energies had been released, the angels filled up the area with a divine healing energy (the patient intuitively knowing the colour), as one cannot take something away without putting something back in its place (as nature abhors a vacuum). It is at this stage that any elemental spirits, or negative animal, bird or insect influences that have become attracted to the surplus of negative emotion are also released in the same way, together with any other influences that may be there as a result of negative past associations. Again the area is flooded with divine energy. The solar plexus area becomes more energised and is now prepared for the healing of the psychic injuries, which in this case were the sword wound from the past life as a soldier and the bruising from the car accident in the present life.

The patient's Guardian Angel was called upon to help to heal the solar plexus, also a special angel that resided within that area. They healed all the damaged tissue in the solar plexus, including the skin, tissue and muscles in the surrounding area. All the psychic bruising was healed, leaving the skin feeling more alive and vibrant.

After the psychic injuries had been healed by the angels, the patient was linked into the special angel in the solar plexus area; the main qualities of this particular angel being strength and courage. The solar plexus then rebalanced itself like a beautiful flower in the early morning sunshine, the aura was also flooded with divine energy and, after releasing further negative influences, the patient was linked into her Guardian Angel within the aura, as well as imbibing its special qualities of love and compassion.

It cannot be ignored that although Psycho-Regression therapy is dealing with the irrational, it is a highly comprehensive, systematised system of healing. And, as the procedure is also very ritualistic, this enables the patient to work 'irrationally' within a framework, enabling him or her to feel safer as well as more secure.

When a priest says the Christian Mass, there is a great deal of ritualistic procedure before the consecration of the bread and wine takes place; at this time transubstantiation occurs (when the bread and wine become the body and blood of Christ). Within the familiarity of this ritual people are able to relax, absorb and quite naturally acknowledge this major process of transformation. They are not overwhelmed by it because of the familiarity of the whole ritual. The same applies to this type of work. People are able to solve their problems through a carefully prepared system that enables them to contact the deepest and most divine parts of the self.

When organs and limbs have been cut out or cut off in different incarnations – for example, head, arms, legs, tongue or genitals removed – then angels bring back the etheric counterparts and rejoin the etheric organ with the rest of the body. A sensitive patient could be aware of this happening, with the particular part of the body becoming stronger as a result. Holes, wounds and tears are also healed up by the appropriate angel.

When organs have been removed through torture or even an operation, then the etheric counterpart is recalled by the patient's higher self until it manifests above the patient's body and is then cleansed by the angels and gradually merges with the physical body lying on the bed until properly realigned and united.

Cuts, burns and skin diseases are cleansed by the angels and then new etheric skin is re-formed; this in turn subtly affects the physical skin (see the case history on pages 160 – 1).

The function of the therapist is as the earthing channel for the angels to do their work, likened to the earth wire in a electrical plug.

General wounds, like axe wounds, arrow, bullet and knife wounds, are cleaned by the angels and checked to make sure there is no remaining part of the etheric weapon in the patient's body; the area is then closed up by the angels. If part of the psychic weapon or instrument remains within the body it is taken out by the angels before they close up the area.

If a person in a previous life has been smothered, drowned or gassed (not an uncommon experience in previous lives during war years, or many centuries ago), any remaining negative energy as a result of the death experience, like the psychic counterpart of earth, water or gas, also has to be removed, as well as the emotional trauma.

If in the past the body has been totally destroyed, blown up or mutilated then the angels reconstruct a new etheric body or draw back the body as it was before it was destroyed by the experience. This can easily be achieved as we are working outside of space and time. The patient always knows which way the etheric body associated with that experience should be reintegrated with the present auric structure. This type of operation strengthens the present aura as well as the physical body.

Brand marks connected with past diabolical pacts or agreements are always broken up and brought to the surface of the skin alongside the negative emotions, and are then released with any other negative influences which may have accumulated there as a result.

Blood pacts or psychic poisons are usually in the blood and this energy has to be brought up to the surface of the whole body. The patient usually sees this type of negative energy manifesting as perhaps a dirty red, brown or black colour. All of the psychic skin structure and the aura is then opened and the negative energy is replaced by a positive energy.

When a heart or other organ transplant has taken place, the patient tunes into the negative energies within the organ from the donor releasing them in the same way in conjunction with his own negative conditions. The angels are then able to heal the organ and to rejuvenate it with spiritual energies which are specially chosen for the particular area.

Strangulation scars are dissolved by the angels and the skin strengthened and rejuvenated.

Crooked spines or limbs created psychically by past injuries are straightened by the angels and corresponding negative emotions and influences are released. When a person undergoes this type of experience, like all other treatment, this can gradually help to strengthen the physical spine.

Martyr wounds, needles, thorns, nails or bullets are broken up and released with the corresponding emotions in the same way as mentioned earlier for 'brand marks'. If any psychic object is left within the body or aura then it is removed by the angels.

There was one woman I saw who was in a lot of physical pain and she found it very difficult to lie comfortably on the therapy couch for any period of time, so I asked the angels to give her a psychic anaesthetic in order to release her from the discomfort. She was asked what colour the anaesthetic was, and it turned out to be a pale blue substance permeating the whole body. After that she was easily able to proceed with the therapy as the anaesthetic did not affect her mind and emotions, only her body.

When a person has been healed of major psychic injuries, the aura always has to be treated as it reflects everything externally that occurs within the physical body. The aura can also be injured separately, often through shock, trauma, excessive use of alcohol, heavy drugs or through electric shock treatment. These cause tears, holes, or very weak areas in the aura. The angels are able to heal all of these things with divine energy once the negative sources of the injury have been dealt with.

During the process of Psycho-Regression it is necessary to understand how an injury occurred and what can be learnt from it, in order to heal the psychic wounds. With general regression these factors are not taken into account or even thought about. This is one of the major differences between the two approaches, Psycho-Regression covering a very much wider spectrum of possibilities within the healing process. These methods have not been written about before to my knowledge, neither in the West nor in the East.

6

RELEASING TRAPPED PARTS OF THE SELF

It is amazing how many parts there are within our self that need to be joined and harmonised before we are able to become whole or holy beings. If more orthodox physicians, psychologists and other physicians of the human psyche really comprehended the effects of unresolved past karma, a great deal more positive action could be undertaken within the more well-known systems of healing. It is not easy for anyone to realise that life is, indeed, a lot stranger than fiction.

Everything on earth is made up of energy, vibrating at different frequencies, depending upon the atomic structural pattern within the atoms and molecules. When these energies are disturbed they become stuck or clogged up like a drain, the energies remaining static until they are finally able to loosen and reform themselves harmoniously. The same thing occurs within an individual's unresolved karmic energies. Like an orchestra we are comprised of many parts, each instrument working harmoniously together in order to create the best possible sound.

Science-fiction writers have an intuitive or possibly

an unconscious understanding of what man experiences within his deepest recesses of the Psyche when they write about people being trapped in other dimensions or time zones. These writers are able to tune into what Dr Carl Jung called 'the collective unconscious', the meeting point outside space and time where all our past, present and future experiences reside within a great universal oneness of life.

Personal integration of different parts of ourselves is really the basis for illumination. In order for us to become a fully integrated, joyful and loving human being we have to really know ourselves. To know ourselves means being able to reconnect with all the different or perhaps lost parts of ourselves that may have got mislaid somewhere along our path towards wholeness.

Space . . . time . . . and reincarnation

Time is man-made and confuses the spirit world greatly, as well as the world of human beings. When psychics attempt to categorise a sequence of events within a given period of time, this can often be very inaccurate, as in the spirit world time does not exist and events take place simultaneously. The well-known spirit guide Seth talks through his medium or channel Jane Roberts about reincarnation happening simultaneously outside of space and time. According to this concept we are not just living one life at a time, but many, conjointly and not sequentially. This is not an easy idea to comprehend intellectually, though I have found during a regression that part of a person's consciousness can be living in another dimension simultaneously.

Even those of us who do believe or intuitively know that reincarnation is a fact, we mostly feel a lot happier with the thought that we live one life at a time, since it seems easier to believe and far less complex, and doesn't cause one to wander into waters that appear to be far too deep even to begin to comprehend. There are, however, no hard-and-fast rules as far as the growth and development of the human psyche is concerned. Whether one lives simultaneously within a number of coexisting incarnations or just in one, it is still necessary to integrate all parts of the self in order for the energies to become integrated enough to enable one to feel really balanced.

Even though time is man-made, there is a space – time continuum that is very real to us. People can and do get their energies trapped between lives, as also in other dimensions or time zones in which they may have lived prior to being on earth. When these energies are reintegrated a person naturally experiences a type of relief that cannot be put into words.

Symptoms and reasons for trapped energies

When someone has a 'missing part', the symptoms can be many and various. The most common feeling is that 'something is missing' in one's life or the person may feel constantly 'spaced out', 'disorientated', 'preoccupied with something else' or they may be longing for something which they cannot quite define.

One young Indian boy, when undergoing regression, re-experienced being in a battle where his head was cut off and also one of his legs. After his death, his spirit was able to look down at his body and saw that his head and leg were disconnected. During the therapy the angels connected the etheric missing parts to his physical present time body. Although his physical body was complete in his present life, he had a weakness in one of his legs, and also problems with his neck and throat, so his experiences in that particular incarnation made intuitive sense to him. During the session the angels reconnected the etheric head to the physical head, and also connected the missing leg. During that particular past life experience he had been a deeply religious person and was very disturbed when he was buried in unconsecrated ground. These two unresolved conditions caused his spirit to remain trapped within the vibrations of that trauma. Once the psychic injuries were healed, and the missing parts reintegrated through Psycho-Regression, he was then able to feel a lot more 'in the body' and connected to his energies within his present life experience.

Although a person's spirit is usually freed from the physical body after death, the way that a person dies, in conjunction with his or her emotional and psychic state, has a great bearing on his or her next incarnation. The Buddhists say that the manner in which a man leaves one life indicates how he will continue with the next; which means that there are strong karmic implications which could either help or hinder the next existence.

Buddhists endeavour to help the complete release of the spirit after death through regular chanting and prayers. Many Catholics perform a requiem Mass for the release of the departed soul, without perhaps comprehending the inner ramifications of such a request. Within most religions and religious systems there are a number of different ceremonies and prayers for the spirits of the dead, which helps them to overcome any possible trauma following the death of the physical body.

RELEASING A SPIRIT
FROM ANCIENT EGYPT

There was a man who felt that 'something was missing', and he was regressed back to a life in ancient Egypt when he was a high priest in one of the temples there. He held an important position within the hierarchial structure of the temple and therefore exercised a lot of power. He was a very dedicated person and did not try to please the pharoah by agreeing with everything that he said, and he was surrounded by a lot of jealousy and resentment from people who were only too willing to usurp his position. He did not approve of the worship of many of the gods and over a period of time he was gradually poisoned by his enemies, so that he became very weak as well as deeply saddened by the people around him in their bid for personal power when he just wanted the best for Egypt.

It was the custom of the time to remove organs from the body after death, and when he died he had various organs removed and put into special jars. A herbal solution was then put into the body to preserve it and he was enbalmed with the many bandages of mummification. During the process of the bandaging spells were secretly incorporated into the folds of the linen in order to trap the spirit and prevent it from reincarnating. The man was ritually cursed and a black magic ceremony was performed over the body before he was officially put into his sarcophagus.

During the regression, through the help of the angels, he then reconnected with the trapped spirit within the mummified form . . . which, interestingly enough, has not been excavated yet. Then the angels opened the bandages to release the spirit of the Egyptian priest that had been trapped for thousands of years through black magic. The spirit was then drawn back until it was above the man's physical body lying on the bed in present time. After the psychic counterpart had

123

been thoroughly cleansed by the angels, the Egyptian spirit was then reintegrated with the Englishman. The positive aspect *of this spirit embodied power and wholeness.*

In order to complete this healing process the angels then released the psychic organs from the jars, reintegrating them into the physical organs of his present-day existence. The effect of this strengthened his individual organs and increased his general physical health and well-being.

The long-term effect of incorporating these missing parts and linking again with the trapped part of himself enabled him to develop his inner potential, as well as feeling a lot more centred within the physical body. He realised that he really needed to know why he had unconsciously put himself into the role of being a 'victim'. This was connected with other aspects of past unresolved karma to do with 'guilt', and he was unconsciously punishing himself in the Egyptian incarnation and also in his present life.

TRAPPED UMBILICAL ENERGY

There was the case of a young man who felt extremely hypocritical about having to pretend to the world at large that he enjoyed being male, when he felt quite the reverse. During the course of therapy he travelled inwardly to the weakest part of his body, the umbilical area, which reflected his problems in this particular incarnation. The trapped energies were partly caused by his 'fear of living on earth', 'emotional shock' and 'fear of being in a male body'. This was to do with incarnating into a male body when a female body would have been strongly preferred.

He had also experienced a number of incarnations on other planets, when he had not been limited by his overt sexuality, being androgynous and possessing a much lighter kind of luminescent body. He had also experienced a number of lives on earth when he had many happy memories of being in a

124

female body. He had no recent happy memories of a male existence. These energies were released from the umbilical area with the help of the angels, then he was able to travel back into another existence when he had really been happy as a man and he had enjoyed being in this particular kind of body.

The combination of these two important aspects brought about a great deal more self-acceptance, and he was able to acknowledge his own maleness without the strong, unconscious reservations that had prevented him from enjoying life to the full. He became a lot more extrovert and was able to form more meaningful relationships.

TRAPPED ENERGIES MEANS UNFINISHED BUSINESS

When parts of the self become trapped in other dimensions, this always indicates that there is something that the person has not yet integrated or understood. A negative action could engender a strong guilt reaction which is usually amplified by existing weaknesses within the person's psychic-genetic imprint.

One woman had low self-esteem and felt that she was really ugly. She regressed back to Germany to the 5th century BC, where she felt herself to be a deformed man with a large head, and small hands and feet. Because of this deformity he was hung up in a cage in the city centre for all to see and to ridicule, and after a great deal of physical and emotional suffering he died in the cage.

After reliving this death the woman released the loneliness and the feelings of ugliness and hatred connected with that past personality. And in this life she felt that the lesson she had learnt from the experience was that any type of differences in people can create problems, and can tear one apart. Even after her death she knew that it was the 'hatred' of people

125

that had inwardly trapped her energies into that particular time zone, distorting the psychic-genetic imprint, and therefore creating a disturbance within the auric structures in her present life. For example, her hatred had created psychic deformities within the spinal and skeletal structure, yet once the angels had healed the psychic injuries her spine was straightened, her skeletal system harmonised, and the arms, legs and head were realigned. It was bitterness and resentment connected with a lost love in a previous incarnation which had brought about such a strong reaction in this one.

When this woman was able to love and accept herself, she really began to enjoy her life in the present time, almost feeling reborn after the release of the hatred and all of the demons, spirits and negative energies connected to that particular life. She needed to learn that hate deforms, drains and eventually kills in one form or another.

OUT OF TIME

Another woman became trapped in another time zone because of 'stubborness', 'emotional rigidity' and 'fear of letting go'. She regressed back in time to when she was a 24-year-old man who thought he was in love, but the girl's family did not want them to see each other as he came from a poorer background. They arranged to meet at night by a river, and when she did not turn up, he felt abandoned, rejected and his pride was obviously hurt. He vowed never to see her again and he never did. He remained unmarried and at the age of 50 he still thought about her, feeling very angry and cheated in his love. At 60 he lost the will to live, still feeling that she was the only one who ever understood him. Sadly he died. After leaving the body he realised that he had wasted his life through his stubbornness and fixed ideas on how life should have been.

Negative emotions that were released connected to this experience included 'fear of letting go', 'feelings of being abandoned', 'rejected', 'boredom with life', 'feelings of waiting', 'stubbornness', 'fear of new beginnings', 'lack of belief in positive change' and 'emotional rigidity'.

After the regression, as a young woman in this life she stopped looking for Mr Perfection and became a lot more realistic and down-to-earth about her emotional relationships, and less demanding. She had become 'out of time' with the realities of life because she had grown out of tune with herself, and this experience brought her into a much more intimate connection with her true feelings.

TRAPPED THROUGH GUILT

A Swedish woman regressed back in time and found part of herself wandering in a graveyard with terrible feelings of guilt, desperation and despair. As a court judge (male) in that particular incarnation she had wrongly accused a young girl of stealing, and the girl was convicted and sentenced to death. In total desperation, guilt and remorse the judge killed himself, pushing an arrow into his heart. He was buried in the same graveyard as the girl and he was unable to leave because of his feelings of guilt. After the regression, the following emotions were released: 'desperation', 'loneliness', 'guilt', 'lack of understanding' and 'suicidal feelings'. The angels took the arrow head out and healed the heart, then the spirit was drawn back and reintegrated.

HAUNTED BY PAST REMORSE

A South African woman was trapped in another time zone because of a murder which she had committed in another century. She was regressed to being a poor man living in the Andes, where he had to search for his food in order to survive. One night he went to a small village and broke into one of the local houses. He was just about to steal some food when a young girl of about 10 saw him and shouted for help. Without a great deal of reflection and with the instinct of a hungry animal, he killed the girl with a knife, took the food and ran away.

When the South African woman came back into present time after the regression, she was still very shocked that she had done such a thing. Although she had released the guilt feelings of 'deprivation', 'self-hate' and 'murderous feelings' associated with the experience, she still felt a great deal of unaccountable remorse connected to herself, as well as to her relationship with God. In this case it was necessary to regress her again in order for her to make peace with God through the receiving of absolution.

The receiving of absolution

One really does not have to be an orthodox religious person in order to be absolved of one's sins. The word *sin* means trangression of the divine law, wrongdoing or offence. Absolution, generally speaking, is a formal forgiveness or remission of sins, and is considered by many religious people to be a sacrament. The word absolution stems from the Latin *absolvere* meaning to free or acquit, and *solvere* to loosen or solve.

A person can be absolved and loosened from past life transgressions, *after* he has been regressed and has understood the reasons for his actions, and released the negative emotions and psychic conditions that he may have accumulated through a number of lifetimes. Only then is the patient ready to receive absolution.

The practitioner lays hands upon the patient's head and calls upon the divine energy that is most appropriate for the individual. If the person is a Christian the practitioner may call upon Christ, or the Madonna, St Francis or another Christian saint; if the patient is a Muslim then the power of Allah will be invoked; or the practitioner may call upon the divine energy the patient really feels comfortable with. The therapist then anoints the top of the patient's head with sacred oil, opening the crown chakra (see Glossary), and with a concentrated divine intention links strongly into the required divine source of energy.

During this procedure the practitioner becomes a vehicle for the divine energy in order for it to flow harmoniously in through the head into the arms and out through the hands into the patient's body, repeating the words of absolution out loud for the patient to hear, and then chanting sacred sounds appropriate to the divine moment. The patient usually feels a warm energy flowing gently through the whole body, and can only genuinely accept this forgiveness after the guilt and other negative emotions have first been released.

During the receiving of absolution the patient may inwardly see an embodiment of one of the sacred energies present, like an angel, spiritual helper or guide. Occasionally patients have seen the figure of Christ or Buddha transmitting the divine energy through the medium of the practitioner.

Even when a person has released the negative energies and received absolution, he or she may still need to talk about their feelings in order to forgive themselves totally for their past actions. A good example of this was a woman who in a past life had been a cannibal in the Borneo jungle and she ate human flesh. A thousand years ago this was permissible and socially acceptable. However, she broke the taboo of the time and ate some babies from her own tribe. This was totally unacceptable and she was ritually killed by the tribe for her misdemeanour. After regression the woman released the negative emotions connected with this experience and received the absolution. She also had therapy for her 'emotional shock' connected with the realisation of her past actions. After this experience it was very necessary for her to realise that we are all evolving and that her consciousness and morality from over a thousand years ago was naturally very different from her present-time understanding and awareness. She had to realise that we all go through many past negative as well as positive experiences in order to achieve oneness with God, and that negative judgement plays no constructive part in this process of transformation. When she realised that neither God nor the practitioner had judged her, she was then able to forgive herself inwardly. This self-acceptance broke down the remaining barriers connected with this experience, thereby releasing a trapped part of herself that had not been able to surface, due to deeply embedded guilt connected with the past.

Being trapped through ecstasy and bliss

We can just as easily be a prisoner of ecstatic and blissful past life experiences, which can sometimes be even more difficult to come to terms with than the negative counterpart. We tend to hang on to what is harmonious and blissful, even in our present life, often becoming so attached to the source of our bliss or ecstasy that we cease to learn from the experience until some event comes along to teach us about letting go of our attachment to pleasure, as well as to the avoidance of pain, in order for us to experience more easily an inner freedom and peace that lies somewhere beyond the opposites which we studiously try to avoid. Many of the old Japanese

Samurai films portrayed graphically the pleasure/pain principle within the blissful state of ecstatic love, and the pain of a dishonourable death, yet subtly insinuating a state beyond these opposites. We carry deep within us the painful as well as the pleasurable experiences of our karmic past which resides within the waters of forgetfulness or unconsciousness, only surfacing when a corresponding situation stimulates it into remembrance.

Some people find it extremely difficult to integrate past blissful and ecstatic experiences within their day-to-day existence. For example there was the case of a young man who had experienced a very happy life in China as a woman. In that life she was married to a wealthy merchant, but she had fallen in love with a business associate of her husband's and they had a passionate love affair. However, the business associate thought that the situation was really not very honourable nor diplomatic so he broke up the relationship after just a few months. This devastated the young woman and she spent the rest of that particular life mourning her loss. In his present life as a young heterosexual male, he again met his past love (he also was a man in this life) and he became increasingly emotionally obsessed with him, since meeting him again had rekindled the past brief ecstatic experience. The business associate who had finished the relationship in China broke up the relationship again this time. The devastated young man re-experienced all of the emotions connected with what he considered to be his ecstatic past, and he felt deeply rejected and unwanted. However, he did not let these feelings deter him as he became increasingly convinced that his friend was his soul mate, not appreciating how his friend really felt. The situation became increasingly difficult for many years as the rejected man's obsession did not fade, even with various types of therapy including Psycho-Regression. It was obvious that he had no real desire to relinquish the obsession with this man and his past ecstatic experience. This case also illustrates the fact that if a person is not ready or does not want to change then nothing on heaven or earth can force them to do so, no therapy being effective without the genuine co-operation of the patient and, as we have said, integrating past ecstatic experiences seems to be very difficult for people to come to terms with.

A young man who had once been an angel experienced those past heavenly ecstasies during regression and he found it extremely difficult to accept being a young man on this earth plane. He found young women, in their 20s like him, rather emotionally demanding and materialistic in their attitudes towards life and relationships. He was able to understand something about the true nature of his spiritual roots quite early in this life and, to adapt successfully to living in this world, he attracted a non-materialistic girlfriend and eventually took up healing.

Releasing the trapped spirits of embryos

It is not uncommon for spirits to be trapped within the womb through past and present life experiences. If a woman has had a miscarriage or abortion, or she died before the birth, the spirit could become trapped within the psychic-genetic structure of the embryo. The spirit does not disappear the moment a foetus is terminated, it usually remains embedded within the womb lining, especially if the mother is traumatised by the experience, for her emotional disturbance can keep the spirit firmly connected to her magnetic field unless she is able to release the spirit through meditation and prayer, thereby releasing her emotional attachment. She can collect a number of psychic embryos even in one incarnation if several pregnancies are terminated. However, if the emotional attachment remains unresolved, she can carry these spirits with her into a number of other incarnations until they are finally released. If, on the other hand, she works through her emotions connected with the termination or miscarriage, then the spirit will be able to be freed in order to continue with the next phase of its evolution.

There are women who are very attached to their unborn child, weaving fantasies around 'what might have been', thereby creating what are generally known as *phantom pregnancies*. This is an excellent name for them, for this is what they really are. Some of these unborn spirits still have a great desire to be born, and with a mother's unresolved energies they attempt to go through the gestation period. This is why a woman's abdomen can swell up and she can look quite pregnant. When a woman is diagnosed as having a phantom pregnancy, the condition is not usually treated with the proper respect and compassion that it deserves.

There was a case of a young woman in her early 20s who was a virgin. Her abdomen kept on swelling up at regular intervals, so she consulted her doctor and was told in a rather dismissive way that she was imagining it all and that she 'just had a phantom pregnancy'. She was not given any psychiatric help, and even if she had been it would have taken a considerable length of time to get her to the stage of releasing her attachment to embryos connected to another incarnation. In a recent life she had been tortured in a concentration camp and she had lost twins, and in a life prior to that one she had practised a satanic form of sexual magic and in a very early incarnation she had lost a baby that she really wanted, and still carried a great deal of grief regarding that experience. All these unresolved experiences added up to many psychic embryos needing to be released, as well as all of the deeply buried emotional trauma, past black magic and links with Satan.

After she had re-experienced these past life conditions, she was able to release the grief, guilt and other corresponding emotions, as well as the past black magic and satanic links. When all of this had been completed and the womb was vibrant with divine light and energy, she was linked into the angel protecting the womb area and was then ready to release the spirits trapped within the psychic embryos.

The womb chakra was opened and, with the four archangels and her own Guardian Angel protecting her body and aura, the practitioner called upon the angels to lift the psychic embryos out of the womb in order for them to be free to reincarnate. At this moment the young woman needed to overcome any subtle reluctance to release the spirits trapped within the psychic embryos, then at the point of inner surrender the four Archangels gently lifted the trapped spirits out of the womb, simultaneously releasing them into the light. The patient often feels a deep inner peace as the spirits are taken by the angels, the womb is then flooded with divine light energy, and the patient connected to the angel that protects it. Afterwards the womb chakra quite naturally rebalances itself, and the psychic skin structure in the womb area closes. This process is helped by the angels and the therapist, thereby amplifying the process of inner visualisation.

Men have, of course, been women in previous incarnations though usually this type of regression and releasing of embryos does not occur when a person has a physical male body. If such a problem exists within the male then it usually remains dormant within the psychic-genetic structure until he incarnates into a female body. If this type of problem manifests within a man at all it usually reveals itself on the mental level through 'jealousy of pregnant women' or 'suppressed unfulfilled desires for pregnancy' which are usually very hidden. These desires sometimes reveal themselves within a transvestite male who dresses up as a female ... The reasons for this can be many and varied, including an unconscious wish to become pregnant.

There are many ways in which parts of the self can become trapped due to unfinished business connected with other lifetimes. Acts of indiscretion brought about by wrong thoughts, words or deeds against others simultaneously affect us.

When we hurt others we always hurt ourselves, as beyond limitations of space and time, within the very heart of God, we really are all one. We stumble from one life into another trying to understand this in many different ways, often taking thousands of incarnations for us just to realise this simple truth, creating great gaps between the divine essence and what we perceive to be reality. It is really amazing how we create prisons for ourselves in our pursuit of divine freedom.

7

SEXUAL REGRESSION

Many different types of emotional, spiritual and monetary problems can affect our everyday existence. However, one of the most poignant areas of disturbance is in our sexual lives. We often 'put up with this' because we do not usually know how to locate the real source of the problem which may have been smouldering away in the unconscious recesses of the mind and body for a very long time. People are not generally aware that they can release karma from previous existences, let alone understand the unresolved problems connected to their sexual karma.

The sex force is a *life force* and if we have a problem with the expression of our sexuality, then this reveals to us that we have an imbalance that reflects itself within every aspect of our life. We first have to admit that we have a problem, even if it is only initially to ourselves. The inner desire for change needs to be very strongly motivated before any lasting transformation starts to take place within our outer lives. Our sex lives clearly reveal to us the symptomatic picture of more deeply buried sexual problems, for example we may have a sexual phobia, or desire too much sex or too little, or be unable to express our deep inner love in an uninhibited and natural way.

Symptoms of sexual trauma

It is unusual to meet a person with a perfectly harmonious sex and love life on every level – sexual, emotional, mental as well as spiritual. When a person forms a close relationship at least one or more of these levels is actively operational. A couple may have a reasonably harmonious sexual relationship and also share similar interests. The relationship may satisfy their basic needs, although their interaction may not be strongly passionate or spiritually stimulating as their understanding of spiritual matters may be worlds apart or even lying dormant in the subconscious. When the sexual experience is separated from the process of loving, a person may feel that he or she is 'having a good time' and may not be consciously aware that there is an important ingredient missing within the relationship.

There was a young woman who had a relationship with five different men at the same time: she had a physical/sexual relationship with a boxer, a stimulating mental relationship with an art historian, a creative relationship with an artist, an intellectual relationship with a philosopher and a light-hearted relationship with a man who just enjoyed having fun and not taking life too seriously. She was able to enjoy all of these relationships, only receiving what each one of them were able to give to it, without imposing upon them any impossible ideals to live up to. She had learnt to appreciate the positive qualities within her five men friends and at the same time was enjoying a lively, down-to-earth sexual relationship with the boxer. Years later she fell in love and experienced a much more satisfying and integral relationship as she was then able to express herself more openly on the physical, mental and emotional levels. However, she still appreciated the importance of her friends who had helped her during her process of unfoldment.

We need friends to help us to bring to the surface of our consciousness many different and fascinating aspects of ourselves that rarely have the opportunity to surface with only one relationship, although this is certainly possible. If this does happen and there *is* a dynamic connection on all levels, the relationship could be thought of as a divine gift from the heavenly worlds or possibly a living demonstration of the laws of positive karma in action.

Many people in personal sexual relationships can block one another off from experiencing relationships with other people, and because of their own insecurities they live in one another's pockets instead of allowing their love to flow outwards to all of the people in their environment. We have all seen couples at parties clinging to one another, instead of making new friends and sharing their ideas and views on life. When a relationship becomes a prison this shows that there is a very strong underlying trauma that reveals itself as 'sexual and emotional insecurity'. If these emotions remain unchanged they just become more deeply embedded, emotionally choking the people involved, gradually destroying the relationship regardless of any good intentions.

There are many manifestations or symptoms of sexual trauma, but those that seem to come up most often can be put into the following categories.

1. Sexual craving

If a person manifests sexual craving they never feel satisfied, no matter how many times they have sex.

This is often due to an extreme craving for a contact that is very much deeper than the physical act of sexual intercourse, and is often connected to very deep sources of emotional pain and inferiority.

There are naturally many reasons why a person never feels sexually fulfilled, although they almost always stem from very much deeper feelings of lack of fulfilment, often connected with relationships in other lifetimes. All sources of sexual trauma are connected with unresolved past events.

On the physical level there may be some hormonal imbalance, including an overactive endocrine system. The deep-seated emotional anguish and craving affects and confuses the reactions of the physical body, not the other way round as is often thought.

Sexual craving could be partially caused if a person dies during a pleasurable sexual experience, like a man who was happily married and living with his wife and children in Italy at the time when Mount Vesuvius erupted. He was making love with his wife when the volcano erupted and the molten lava came down the mountain killing them all. During another life, this time as a woman, she was making love when her lover was taken as a prisoner, and she never saw him again. In a more recent incarnation as a woman she was sexually tortured for not revealing the names of persons suspected of witchcraft during the inquisition. Therefore, in two lives this man had died at a time of sexual pleasure, and in another life he experienced being tortured sexually, so it was not really surprising that he could not respond without overreacting sexually in his present life.

During therapy all of the traumatised emotions, including 'emotional shock' and 'craving', needed to be released from the body and aura, especially the heart and genitals. After the therapy the sexual craving completely disappeared, and he was then able to feel a great deal more emotionally secure and at peace with himself.

2. Sexual indifference

I have not come across many people who are genuinely indifferent to sex within a loving context. There are very few celibates around who never think about sex nor have any form of sexual need or desire. I have met many young men in spiritual circles who have declared solidly that they were celibate and expressed this idea a little too often, possibly trying to convince themselves of this, working with the old-age conditioning that being celibate is a lot more spiritual than being in a harmonious and loving relationship. I once worked with a priest who declared that he was celibate, although he masturbated from time to time, which he felt was rather a nuisance, though he still considered himself to be above the lusts of the flesh. He suffered a great deal of guilt as a result of his actions.

There are also men and women who do not feel a lot of satisfaction during lovemaking, so they gradually detach themselves from their sexual desires and physical needs.

One woman I knew was only able to relax completely once or twice a year when she was on her summer holiday and had had a few drinks. The rest of the year she remained sexually uninterested in her spouse, her sexual energies actively manifesting themselves in her sharp tongue and her highly idealistic attitudes towards life, which no one could really hope to live up to, least of all her husband.

When people appear to be sexually indifferent they are usually harbouring a great deal of frustration and anger on deeper levels of their being, which could affect several areas of, or even their whole body. There are always much deeper emotions that lie behind the surface. 'Indifference' needs to be treated before the more deep-seated emotions like 'pain', 'fear of failure', 'sexual guilt', 'repulsion' or some other specific core emotion can be released.

One always needs to understand if there is any negative parental conditioning involved, then the therapist can regress the person to understand what this deep-seated sexual conditioning is really all about and to come to terms with it. This will not only release their own negative emotions, but also the emotions of their parents. (See the section on surrogate regression, page 155.)

People can sometimes be thought to be sexually indifferent just because their own natural sexual rhythm is only stimulated into activity during specific phases of the lunar cycle. The truth is that everyone has very different sexual and emotional needs. For example, one man stated that he was highly active sexually, which to him meant once a month, while another man said that he was not very sexually active as he only wanted sex five times a week, and yet another man felt that he really needed to ejaculate several times a day in order to feel free from sexual tensions.

Too much or too little sexual desire indicates that there is an imbalance within the psyche that needs to be rectified. Everyone's sexual rhythm is unique and is also dependent upon other factors like personal stress, the environmental situation and also the emotional output. The once-a-month man may take approximately 28 days to build up his sexual energies to their maximum potential. He may be very active in his job and be putting out a lot of energy, so his sexual activity at this specific time may be much more powerful orgasmically than many more superficially experienced ejaculations. The man or woman who experiences sexual activity may often have quantity but not necessarily quality.

141

The bodily rhythms become more finely attuned and stabilised when a person has worked on or at least understood some of the psychic effects of his or her sexual past from other lifetimes.

3. Sexual dislikes or repulsion

If a person has very strong anti-feelings about sexual activity, this indicates that there is something unresolved within the karmic sexual pattern which may stem from early childhood problems in this life, from attitudes of the mother and father or from another incarnation.

There was the case of a young woman who did not like to be touched by her husband and even found it difficult to hug her children. She was regressed back to another life in the 18th century when she was a young serving maid of about 14 years of age and worked in a large country manor. During one lazy summer's afternoon when her employers were out she was wandering around the very large grounds, when one of the stable boys called her to come and look at the beautifully groomed horses in their stables, which she did. On entering the stables the boy slammed the large wooden doors shut and then proceeded to attack and sexually assault her. During the regression she vividly relived the whole experience, even trying to get away from her aggressor and wiping her clothes clean after he had left the stables.

This was an emotionally traumatic experience for her and she cried a lot. She then released all of the negative emotions connected with the experience of 'sexual repulsion', 'disgust', 'fear', 'anger', 'hate', 'shame' and 'emotional shock'. She also had to find out why she had put herself in the role of the 'victim' in that particular life experience, realising that she unconsciously engineered this due to past sexual guilt when she had misused her sexual powers and personal authority in past lifetimes.

Within a few weeks she became a lot more physical and affectionate with her husband and children. Her husband even felt suspicious as he thought that it was too good to be true. They had been seeing a marriage guidance counsellor and when the counsellor phoned them to find out why they had not been for counselling, they told her that they no longer had a problem. The wife told the counsellor that she had been regressed back into another incarnation where she had experienced being raped, and she had released the emotions connected with the trauma. The counsellor was quite taken aback and did not know what to say. She just murmured a numb 'Yes, that's good' and put the phone down (probably in disbelief!). However, the woman's condition did not recur and she experienced a very much happier and more harmonious sex and emotional life in her marriage, and her children had a much more cuddly, affectionate mother.

Sexual repulsion can be caused by many unresolved past life experiences connected to torture, humiliation, deprivation or satiation to name but a few possibilities.

4. Giving and receiving

Problems with erection, ejaculation and orgasm are all connected with giving and receiving. Even in this life's experiences a person can have a deeply rooted unresolved problem connected with their mother and father who a vulnerable and sensitive child quite naturally uses as a role model.

We all choose our path of destiny before we incarnate according to the areas within our psyche that need to be developed and integrated with the rest of our karma. Our higher self may decide to be reborn in order to begin to understand a little more about the true meaning of 'unconditional love', the 'art of gentleness', 'humility', 'non-attachment' or perhaps to learn to rely on our own inner resources through developing our inner strength.

We have usually known our parents and other members of our family in several previous incarnations before our present life, though often within a totally different context. Sometimes the same person will be a relative, husband, wife, enemy or friend. This enables us to understand more clearly why these primal relationships are so important as they are reflected in our attitude to ourselves, our sexuality and to the world around us. We also have to learn from our parents' present-day attitudes, as well as subconsciously assimilating our past life experiences.

There was a young woman who had rather an emotionally detached relationship with her mother; they were never really very close and the woman could not really fathom out why they were not more affectionate towards one another. This affected her relationship with her own femininity, and she acted rather like a young girl in her early teens instead of a mature married woman in her late 20s. When she was regressed she went back to being a three-month-old foetus in her mother's womb in this life. During early pregnancy her mother was experiencing emotional problems within her marriage and was in a dilemma as to whether to have a baby or not, and after going through a great deal of soul searching and emotional anguish she decided to have an abortion. The growing foetus felt emotionally frozen by her decision and fearfully doomed. The process of the termination had just started when the mother suddenly changed her mind. It was a very sudden decision and no matter what, she would have the baby after all. The little foetus naturally felt a deep sense of relief, but did not relinquish the 'emotional trauma' or the 'feelings of isolation'.

After re-experiencing the nine months in the womb through regression and releasing the negative emotions, the young woman's relationship with her mother completely altered and they became much closer. She also emotionally bloomed like a flower in the springtime, becoming much more centred within her own developing feminine energies.

There was another case of a woman who was regressed back into her mother's womb in this life, to when she was a developing foetus inside the womb and she realised that she was emotionally burdened by her mother's emotions of fearfulness and sexual anxiety. This problem manifested itself in her late 20s, in all of her muscles and joints, making her feel sexually tense and unable to relax properly in order to enjoy a harmonious sex life. After she had relived this experience, releasing her mother's negative emotions as well as her own, she was able to express herself more openly and enjoy a far more harmonious sex life.

The relationship we have with our mother and father strongly connects us to the mother and father of all life, or the masculine and feminine side of God, so it is of prime importance and naturally affects every aspect of our lives, including all of our bodily systems and our energy meridians, and how we think, relate, laugh, pray and love. We need to rediscover how we can best give and receive, both being of equal importance. When one has learnt to understand and perhaps to forgive our parents in this life, we then begin to express ourselves in a very much more human and loving way, quite naturally melting all barriers of dissension.

5. Hypersensitivity or 'deadness' of the sexual organs

If any part of the body is exceptionally hypersensitive, feels strangely 'dead' or unpleasantly overreacts to touch, this tells us that the area or organ holds a lot of unresolved karmic conditions within the psychic-genetic pattern of the area, which could also affect the whole body. Unresolved emotional trauma from the past or present life is held within the tissues or muscular system, and can be greatly helped through Reichian or biodynamic massage (see Glossary) which helps some of the deeply buried emotional traumas to surface.

Dr Wilhelm Reich, who lived in the early 19th century, spent many years researching the effects of sexual repression and its detrimental effects that can occur within a non-orgasmically functioning person. Dr Reich discovered that when a person was sexually traumatised they developed a muscular armouring which stopped the free-flowing psychic energy enabling them to be in a natural receptive state orgasmically. He discovered that when there was an overload of unresolved emotion located in a particular area of the body, this occurred mainly in the pelvic or genital area. He found that either a feeling of 'deadness' occurred or 'extreme feelings of hypersensitivity'. His research took him into the biophysical and emotional areas of sexual imbalance. He used various respiratory techniques and excitation of the retina with light, as well as using specially designed medical equipment like 'orgone accumulators'.

Orgone energy is primordial cosmic energy which can be visually demonstrated by means of a Geiger-counter. With the invention of the orgone energy accumulator this energy became usable. Physical orgone energy concentrated in an orgone accumulator increases the natural bio-energetic resistance of the organism against disease. Reich was able to help people with these revolutionary methods of his day, although he did not encompass the more subtle psychic dimensions of his patients connected with past and present-day karma. Through his writings and researches he presented a new level of awareness to the early 20th century, giving people a much greater opportunity to come to terms with the Victorian sexual leftovers of their forefathers, enabling them to live more orgasmically.

Hypersensitivity or a feeling of deadness directly in the sexual organs was doubtless treated indirectly through the muscular and vegetative system by Dr Reich, for he would have probably been accused of sexual indecency if he had proceeded in any other manner. His main concern was to release trapped energies in the body that were blocking orgasmic functioning, uncovering the emotions connected with the trapped energy which had been brought about in this life. Past life memories trapped in the body were not one of the areas that were covered in his published research.

With Psycho-Regression it is possible to travel inwardly directly into the reproductive organs to the source of sexual trauma, without the patient experiencing any feelings of reticence or shyness as the whole procedure is an inner experience.

One woman who experienced hypersensitivity of the clitoris travelled into that area and found herself in Africa in a recent incarnation. About to experience a clitorectomy, she released 'anger', 'resentment' as well as 'physical and emotional pain connected to the experience'. The area was then filled with divine light energy, followed by the angels healing the area, the hypersensitivity then greatly decreased and she was able to experience erotic sexual sensations more pleasurably.

A man who experienced oversensitivity of the penis and premature ejaculation regressed back to another life when he was tortured and had his genitals removed, and he released negative emotions of 'rage', 'anger', anguish', 'emotional and physical pain' and many past black magic connections, including 'a curse on love'. After rebalancing the area with divine light energy, the psychic organs from that particular incarnation were drawn back and cleansed by the angels. He also needed to release other emotions connected with experiences from his present life, like 'fear of failure' and 'fear of love'. After this the oversensitivity gradually decreased, and he was able to live a more fulfilling sex life.

A woman who had an emotionally 'dead' pelvic area had difficulties experiencing orgasm as well as problems connected with bearing children, having experienced two miscarriages. During regression she went back to a life in the early Americas when she was a young Indian girl of about 13, and she fell in love with a young white male and had sex with him, much to the consternation of her tribe. The fact was that during those times it was taboo for a young maiden to have sex with a white male, so she was ritually put to death. She was strapped to a wheel and ripped in half tearing apart the reproductive organs, as well as splitting the rest of her body.

During this session she released many negative emotions associated with this experience. The angels then had to perform massive psychic surgery on her body, reconstructing the psychic womb and vagina connected with that life as well as healing all of the internal organs, tissues and bones. The result of this session was a greatly improved sex life and a pregnancy that was carried to term.

6. The Don Juan complex

Some people think they are enjoying ultimate sexual freedom when they have many and varied sexual relationships on a regular basis, often proudly boasting of their achievements. This seems to occur more with men than with women, as men are often more frank about what they consider to be their conquests and it is far more unusual for a woman to proclaim that she is having sex with a number of men over a short period of time. When a person has this type of attitude, my first question would naturally be, 'What is the problem, and what are they really trying to prove?' Something surely is amiss for anyone to feel that it is necessary to have many brief sexual encounters, since quality rather than quantity is one of the most essential considerations.

The individual is usually harbouring very raw, unresolved emotions like 'fear of being hurt', 'desire for domination or control', 'self-hate or hate of others', also there could be some very deep wounding that may have occurred as a result of several different past and present life emotional and sexual traumas.

In some parts of the world men are allowed to have more than one wife (polygamy) and may take full advantage of their cultural situation, marrying as many women as their bank book will allow them to. There are said to be some remote tribes in Africa where women are allowed more than one husband (polyandry), although this is more unusual and is often associated with a shortage of females. Women who are married into a polygamous culture are conditioned from an early age to accept the situation. They do not usually have the opportunity to experience the difference between the spiritual and emotional intensity of the energies exchanged in a monogamous relationship, as opposed to a polygamous one.

There was a case of a Don Juan in Africa who married twice. Both his wives hated one another and lived in separate houses. Don Juan spent time living in both residences. His first wife never really believed that he would marry twice and felt very unloved, and she lost a great deal of weight as a result. When the Don Juan married again the second wife then became very jealous of the first, and she was so angry about being the 'second wife' that she visited the local witchdoctor who practised a negative form of black magic. The second wife had a few spells put on the first wife to disrupt her life, and generally to cause havoc in her household. The husband was

149

oblivious to all of this, not having any real understanding of the results of his actions and being totally unaware that the situation was causing any problems.

During regression the first wife released many negative emotions connected with her disturbed state, including the 'black magic' and 'curses' that had been put on her by the witchdoctor, also releasing the 'craving for love', 'feelings of rejection', as well as 'desire for power'. She had the wisdom to realise that she had attracted this situation to her in this life in order to be able to blend unconditional love with wisdom. Through changing her attitude she became a stronger person, enabling her to see her life and her relationship through totally different eyes. The relationship does not finish with a happy-ever-after, but doubtless she will come to the conclusion that is right for her as she continues through her process of unfoldment. She managed to create a very positive inner foundation out of a very confused cultural situation.

I really do not think that the husband (the Don Juan) ever thought that there was anything he needed to do to alter his life or anyone else's, as he had not really experienced the mergence of mind, emotions and body that can occur between two human beings who are deeply in love. One can only surmise that this may be something that he will eventually come to terms with in another incarnation, perhaps within a different cultural setting. It takes a very unusual soul to comprehend the sometimes complex emotions, deep-seated feelings and gut reactions that may lie way beyond what is considered to be the cultural or social norm.

There was a case of a young man from Yugoslavia who was deeply in love with himself and who used to look lovingly in the mirror at every available opportunity. He also loved women and had as many light-hearted, casual sexual relationships as possible without any real involvement. When he went back in time through regression therapy he travelled to another life where he had served in a harem as a eunuch (a castrated male). In an incarnation prior to that he had been a young Inca woman having had his heart ritually taken out in order to appease the Gods. He released many negative emotions as a result of re-experiencing these two incarnations, also becoming inwardly visually aware that his psychic heart and genitals were missing from his auric bodies.

After the negative emotions and psychic conditions had been released in both areas, the angels performed psychic surgery on the organs, cleansing them, merging and integrating them with the physical organs of present time. Several weeks after the therapy he became a lot calmer, more self-assured and far less obsessive, realising that he did not have anything to prove to anyone, least of all himself.

7. Sexual superiority complex

There are quite a number of people who consider them-selves to be 'spiritual' (having very definite notions of what they mean by that word) and who refrain from any kind of sexual relationship. This type of person is not sexually indifferent, but feels that he or she really is a superior being and therefore does not need sex. I am not referring to the rare, genuine celibate who just does not think about sex, but to those who think that they are beyond what they consider to be such a low form of physical activity. Their attitude can be a lot more subtle than described, although the result remains the same – no sex!

Because of religious conditioning and bias they think that if their seed is spilt, they will suddenly become weak and devoid of energy, not knowing through their own personal experience that when sex takes place within a loving context it rejuvenates the physical, emotional, mental and spiritual bodies.

Many young men go through a phase of fantasising about being a yogi or a holy man, often putting themselves through a long period of self-enforced celibacy, breaking out of this mode when their sexuality starts to consume them, becoming a little less rigid and more flexible spiritually and physically. Women tend to withdraw more dramatically when they follow this path of sexual abstinence, often channelling their sexual energies into a sublimated form of ambition or imagining themselves to be 'exceptionally spiritual'. As Ogden Nash put it in his poem 'The Seven Spiritual Ages of Mrs Marmaduke Moore':

> *for when a lady is badly sexed,*
> *God knows what God is coming next.*

I have met several men who think they are the Christ and a few women who think that they are the Virgin Mary, or Mary Magdalenes, but interestingly enough no Buddhas or Mohammeds, and no one has yet claimed to be the reincarnation of Judas or Hitler. When people suffer from sexual superiority they feel that they are important, different and most definitely apart from other mortals. When people have these types of delusions, at the time of regression they have usually had a number of sexually restrained lives like being a monk, nun or a person cut off from general human loving activity. If there have been a sequence of recent incarnations like this, then the individual needs to re-experience them in order to understand why he put himself through such a rigid pattern in the first place.

There was a Frenchman who, when he was a teenager, imagined that he had to be fairly uncomfortable in his home, eat little, not enjoy an occasional drink nor indulge in any form of sexual activity. He felt guilty if he bought any new clothes and he thought that he should not own anything too

152

valuable. He had brought this form of poverty consciousness from his deeply-embedded memories connected with experiences from other lifetimes when he had been a monk, a yogi and a wandering ascetic. He had a very difficult childhood in this life, which had not helped him to alter this particular pattern. He became very much of a recluse, taking up ceremonial magic and occultism later on in life to compensate for the lack of not being able to relate openly in an emotional and sexual way. He did not try to find out why his life was not opening up emotionally for him, not even stopping to wonder why he attracted very few loving relationships. Over the years he channelled all of his sexual and emotional energy into magic and the occult.

At this time he was unaware that when a person amplifies the positive side of their nature, the opposite (negative) also comes to light. As a result of his naïvety all the frustrations, longings and emotional cravings also surfaced, which he found it very difficult to deal with, for he had not taken the purification aspect too seriously, and now he had landed himself in very hot water. The power that he had constantly evoked finally surfaced, bringing up both the positive as well as the negative. Like St George, his dragon had turned up ready for a good fight, but the Frenchman did not have the experience to use his sword or (inner will) to deal with the energy that he had evoked.

When a person evokes and wields power at the expense of the heart, emotions and feelings there is always trouble. The dragon does not just walk away with his tail between his legs; it consumes its opponent.

It is not possible to play charades with what Jung described as the Shadow; total honesty about what is really going on is essential if we are to survive long enough to find out who we really are.

Sexuality is a very important part of our inner

development since it is a very intimate expression of ourselves. With the majority of individuals there are plenty of amazing experiences located within the area of sexual karma. If we were able to see all the different kinds of sexual involvements we have experienced in other incarnations, we would probably reject it out of hand. This is why a person needs slowly to unfold their karmic past, in order to assimilate each piece of the cosmic jigsaw puzzle individually.

8

PSYCHIC DISCOVERIES

I have made many fascinating psychic discoveries through the years during the process of healing and various forms of regression therapy. If the therapist is receptive and open to new information, all sorts of things quite naturally come to light.

About 10 years ago a lot of unusual material surfaced and I began to wonder what else could be revealed. Years later I continue to ask myself that question and extraordinary information still surfaces, perhaps to teach me that there is always more to learn.

Surrogate regression

One wonderful discovery was the realisation that negative energies can be released for another person, through a close friend or relative who has a deep inner understanding of the affected person's needs. For example, a mother may wish to help her baby, or someone who is perhaps too ill to be regressed themselves could be helped by a relative or friend.

Surrogate regression can also be successfully accomplished by a person who has performed negative actions against others in past lives, and wishes to rectify their misdemeanours within their present life. If, for example, one has the power to curse or put a spell on someone, one also has power to release the person *from* that static source of negative energy. The effects of these past actions (which occurred thousands of years ago when the person was full of hate, revenge, jealousy or some other negative emotion) can be nullified. It is very good to know that you can cut through man-made time barriers and neutralise harmful karmic effects created by past deeds performed with negative intention.

A Danish woman had problems relating deeply to her husband; he always seemed to be suspicious of her motives, which left them both feeling frustrated and discontented with their relationship. During regression the woman travelled back to the 13th century in France, where she was the wife of a rich landowner who had an extremely dominant personality which she disliked. She fell in love with a young servant who worked at their chateau; they had an immediate empathy towards one another and met secretly. Within a comparatively short time they started to have an affair, but were quickly discovered by another servant who told his master. The young lover was murdered by the enraged and jealous husband whose ego had been deeply wounded by the whole situation. This left the wife grieving but enraged that her husband had acted so heartlessly and with such revenge.

As the months went past her anger grew more intense until it became rage and abject hatred. A year later her husband became ill almost as though he had inwardly inhaled her fury into his being and he died of a heart attack. On the day of his death, she stood by his grave thanking fate for causing his death and cursing his grave with her vehement hatred. She cursed his spirit, saying that wherever it wandered may it never find rest or experience love to the end of eternity.

Because of his deep-seated guilt at his murderous action his spirit was deeply affected by this curse, and it became trapped between the world of the living and the dead. He was unable to travel forwards or backwards as he was locked within that particular time zone. His ghostly self remained around the grave for 700 years until it was finally released (during a session of Psycho-Regression) by the very same woman who had cursed him. During the regression she realised that the same man was also her husband in her present life and that they had remarried because of their unresolved life in the 13th century. It was no wonder that he was suspicious of her and that there was such a strain in their present-day relationship, she having cursed him so vehemently. When she returned to the graveside in regression and realised that she had trapped part of his spirit through her hate and venom, she asked the angels to help her to release the curses to enable the trapped part of her husband's spirit to return to his present-day body.

She knew inwardly that the curse would be released through her own positive intention during the regression and she also knew without a shadow of doubt that the angels would transform the negative energy, thereby releasing the curse. When this had been successfully achieved the angels were then able to release the trapped spirit, allowing it to reintegrate itself with her husband in this present time. After the regression she did not rush home to tell him all about it, she decided to wait, watch and to see what would happen. Several weeks later he became far more relaxed and at ease with himself as well as with her. He seemed to be far more 'in his body' and less emotionally detached.

Releasing trapped souls connected to a dark past

There was an unusual case of a Spanish woman who was regressed back to Atlantis where she worked in a temple as a priestess of the black arts. Through her satanic practices she deliberately trapped many thousands of souls through her magic, sealing them into crystals which enabled her to draw from their energies at will. When she had therapy, she felt that a static energy was enveloping her like a black cloud, inhibiting her creativity and preventing her from finding a suitable partner in life. There were many emotional problems that needed to be resolved, but the Atlantean life surfaced as one of the major priorities to be dealt with initially, 'desire for power, control and greed' being some of her major weaknesses. After she understood and released the emotions connected to this life, and the motivations that lay behind her actions she felt very much lighter, although inwardly she knew that the session had not been completed. When her body had been rebalanced with divine energies and linked into the angels, she was then ready to release all the souls that had been trapped in the crystals thousands of years before.

She had created this terrible situation through her own past actions and knew that she was the only one able to solve it, with divine guidance. Through the power of God and the angels the crystals which had been petrified in time were broken up and the souls released in order to return to the individuals, whether they be living or dead.

A present-day situation illustrates totally different pos-sibilities for surrogate regression. An Englishwoman who was eight weeks pregnant was very nervous about having another difficult birth, as her first delivery had been a long and painful experience. During Psycho-Regression she went back into another life when she had been crushed by a boulder while pregnant. She also released a number of psychic injuries including spear and knife wounds in the reproductive area. After the therapy her second birth was completely different, going very smoothly. During the course of treatment the mother tuned into the consciousness of the growing embryo, and found that it was a female and that she was suffering from a broken heart from her previous life and that she had committed suicide. After this discovery the mother decided to assist in a surrogate healing for her unborn child. Through guided visualisation, angelic assistance and the mother's love, the broken heart was healed and strengthened, enabling the child to start her life feeling a lot happier.

Clearing the blood

When I was in Kenya many years ago I met a medicine man called Kuzungu, who said that no matter what is wrong with a person the blood must always be treated. Many years later when I was in India, I met the spiritual teacher, His Holiness the late Shri Ram Chandra, who said that no matter what is wrong with a person, the liver must always be cleared. I know that they were both right as the liver and the blood are really one, the liver being a storage house for many of the positive substances within the circulatory system. As with toxins in the bloodstream they pass through the liver and can cause damage and destruction there and throughout the whole system.

The blood is so vitally important because it is the source of life that resides within every part of a person's body, holding the karmic imprint within its psychic cellular structure. Physical blood can be purified in many different ways by natural means, such as a good diet, and through homoeopathic herbs and plants or biochemic salts.

If a person has had a number of major diseases connected with recent previous lifetimes it is possible that the psychic-genetic imprint of these diseases can remain dormant within the blood cells. When the emotional causes of these past diseases are aggravated by corresponding negative emotions connected to present time circumstances, then similar patterns can reoccur within a person's life.

A woman from Somerset came to see me. She was suffering from a very itchy skin, having already taken many allopathic medicines to alleviate this aggravating condition. She had also tried homoeopathic remedies and these had helped her for the longest period of time, although the irritation sporadically continued to recur. During regression she went back to a life when she was a young leper woman in Africa where she was ostracised by her tribe when they found out that she had the dreaded disease. Being a leper in that particular life was a physical symptom of old and unresolved karmic feelings connected with her own mistreatment of others, also self-dislike and guilt. Physical disease is one rather radical way of working off some aspects of negative karma, although it can be worked on a lot more subtly at other levels of consciousness, and through correct thought, word and deed in everyday life.

During the regression she was able to understand the reasons for the leprosy, releasing the corresponding negative emotions from the whole body including 'guilt', 'self-dislike', 'abuse of self and others' and 'hate'. After releasing these emotions from the heart and from the skin over the whole body, she then discovered that these emotions were also in the blood as well as the etheric counterpart of leprosy in the aura.

With the help of the divine energies, her higher self and the angels, and with the use of sacred sounds and rattles, all of this negative energy which she saw as a dirty brown/black colour, left the blood, coming to the surface of her physical body. When it had all collected on the surface of the skin, she then visualised the whole of the psychic skin structure opening throughout the body and the aura, before the angels were called upon to help gently release the negative energies from the blood. The blood and then the body were filled with divine energy and the patient then linked into her Guardian Angel, before cleansing, rebalancing and closing the aura.

Afterwards the negative emotions were released from the body and the blood was physically cleared, also the itchy skin healed. Several months later she became noticeably a lot more light-hearted and felt less burdened now the 'hate' and 'self-dislike' had been released, and her physical health also radically improved.

There was a Dutchman who was a procrastinator, he was also lazy and lethargic, always putting off today what he imagined he could do tomorrow or the day after. He also had a very sluggish physical system including poor circulation. When he decided to find out the cause of his condition through Psycho-Regression he went back to a life when he was a senator in Rome in the 5th century and was one of the personal confidants of the caesar. He was very ambitious and strove cunningly to gain even wider popularity and notoriety. During this brief period of popularity he also dared to have an affair with the caesar's wife, which was a dangerous, even unthinkable thing to do. Unfortunately, this thoughtless and arrogant action led him into very deep waters and he was discovered. This was his total and utter ruin, whereby he would be publicly humiliated and put to death. He decided that it would be better to take his own life rather than to be humiliated, so he poisoned himself, dying a slow agonising death through taking hemlock.

During the regression he released 'arrogance', 'pride', 'desire for power', 'fear of humiliation' and then found that there was a psychic poison in his blood, also a 'suicidal spirit' and a 'demon of self-destruction'. After all these negative influences were released from the blood and the body his circulation improved, enabling him to feel a lot more energetic and vital. He seemed to come alive, initiating positive plans into his everyday life, and he also amazed his friends when he stopped procrastinating.

It is not uncommon for people to have a certain amount of karmic debris in the blood. This can, however, become amplified after a blood transfusion and should be psychically cleansed by natural means. When a sick person receives another's blood, it is not uncommon for the donor to be paying off a karmic debt connected with another lifetime. If one believes that there is no such thing as an accident, this really does not sound extraordinary, but is actually exceedingly logical. If a person's blood has been spilled through violence in the past, the aggressor may get the opportunity to literally return it. This form of divine justice can take place on very physical levels with organ transplants, as well as blood transfusions; or the karmic scales can be balanced on more subtle, mental, emotional and spiritual levels, depending upon the needs of the moment.

If a person who has had an accident and received a blood transfusion has a particularly strong emotional or psychic weakness in his or her makeup, then the psychic energies within the very essence of that blood can take over the personality, even if it is only for a few hours. The blood is the life force and has been used in magic since the beginning of history so it is no wonder that it is a very potent factor, especially when it is introduced into the body of another. This is probably why some religions do not approve of blood transfusions, although I have never seen any convincing argument about the exact nature of their objections, especially from a psychic and spiritual point of view. I feel that one perhaps needs to accept what is offered in a crisis situation and to be thankful for it. If one received blood from another, it can always be purified through one of the natural methods already mentioned. One could also say a little prayer of gratitude for the help given, inwardly asking one's Guardian Angel for extra help and strength during the healing process.

Shrinking obstructions and filling the void

When I was in the Philippines I watched over a hundred psychic operations being performed on the removal of cysts, growths and tumours. I have also seen many psychic operations being performed in Brazil and several in Thailand. I learnt how to watch an operation and not to be impressed by the amount of blood there was. I met some genuine psychic surgeons and also some fake ones, as we find in all walks of life. The fakes had a valid part to play even when they were not able to remove the obstruction, because sometimes people got 'cured' through the placebo effect of the sight of blood during the course of the 'operation'. The genuine surgeons were able to remove physical tissue from the body, much to the relief and delight of many anxious patients.

I had just one question to ask all of these healers and surgeons, during the course of my visits to these places and after spending many hours watching them at work. I really wanted to know how they dealt with the mental and emotional, as well as psychic, conditions that had caused the obstruction in the first place. Some of the surgeons did not even try to come up with an answer as they simply did not know. I asked the well-known psychic surgeon, the late Josephine Sisson, this question and she did not know the answer either. However, she became very interested in the idea of releasing the negative karmic energies associated with cysts, growths and tumours and wanted to investigate this further, but she did not live long enough to accomplish this.

Psychic surgeon Virgilio Gutierrez believed that opening the body was for the non-believers and he said that the obstruction can be made to shrink without breaking the skin. He also tuned into the negative emotions associated with the condition and was able to help the patient emotionally for a time. One woman who was given psychic surgery in the intestinal area by Virgilio was greatly helped, but after approximately three months her condition returned. Several months later the woman had Psycho-Regression and found that many negative emotions still needed to be released. She also found several psychic injuries in the same area, including a dagger wound and the tip of an arrow head. This was the reason why the condition returned. It seems that a person has to take a very active part in their own healing process and not passively expect someone else to do it all for them.

Psychic surgeon, exorcist and healer, David Oligane, knew that negative energies can take the form of witches, low spirits or devils that have to be removed from the patient's body in order to bring about a cure. Through many years' experience as a healer, exorcist and surgeon, he has been able to help many people. However, the same question arises: when the witch, demon, or devil has been taken out of the patient's body, what about releasing the negative emotions that attracted these conditions in the first place? On this David remained silent, but the original negative emotions that act like a magnet, attracting the possessing influence in the first place, also have to be transmuted. This seems to be a major blind spot of all the psychic surgeons I have met in the Far East.

Through this kind of work, it is possible gradually to change the atomic pattern of physical matter and bring the affected part of the body back to its natural vibration, but a person still needs to do a lot of work on him or herself, emotionally, mentally and physically. Patients have been treated with obstructions and have inwardly known that they are getting smaller with the releasing of negative energies. However, we do not have X-rays before and after treatment to prove this yet. Hopefully further research will be done in this area in my lifetime in order to prove this vitally important point scientifically.

One well-known psychic surgeon in Brazil, Odilon da Silva takes X-ray pictures before and after treatment. I was there when an orthodox surgeon from the USA saw the pictures before and after the growth had been removed by psychic surgery. The surgeon was deeply shocked and was really unable to comprehend the situation through his intellect. His confusion grew stronger as he saw many operations taking place and was even allowed to feel the growths melting beneath the surgeon's touch, as well as examine the X-rays. This psychic surgeon's work showed amazing physical results, but like the others he was not aware of what was happening to the primal causes of the sickness or whether the karmic conditions were dealt with effectively.

As obstructions can be shrunk, so voids need to be filled as nature abhors a vacuum. People can walk around with many different types of psychic conditions connected with holes or vacuums.

One woman had a hysterectomy and experienced an acute feeling of emptiness, as well as emotional shock in the womb area. During regression she found that the reason for the removal of her womb in this life was connected to abuse of power in other incarnations, and she then released 'emotional shock', 'despair' and a number of strong emotions that had brought about this physical removal. After the vacuum had been cleared of negative karma, the four archangels and her Guardian Angel reconstructed a psychic womb, filling it with light and energy, reconnecting her to the angel which looked after the womb area. She felt a lot calmer after treatment, and she wrote a letter a few weeks later saying that she was very pleased indeed with her newly-balanced psychic womb. The womb is the chalice of feminine energies so it is important that it is peaceful as well as balanced, even if the physical womb is not present. When the womb is harmonious a woman is usually very creative as well as energetic.

A Finnish woman longed to have a child, and this became so intense that it turned into a craving, becoming a vacuum of frustrated energy turning in on itself in the womb area. This was accentuated by the fact that her husband was unable to produce children and she was not interested in the idea of artificial insemination. She decided to release this intense feeling of emptiness from her womb with Psycho-Regression therapy.

During the session she found out that she had known her husband in another life when they had both mistreated their offspring and had led rather self-centred lives, oblivious of other people's sufferings. During the session she released many of the negative emotions connected with their past selfishness, letting go of all of the deeply buried grief within her womb. Gradually the area began to be re-energised, the vacuum reversing itself and turning into a dynamic energy centre. The couple's relationship began to change as they became a lot more loving towards one another and to the world around them. They did not suddenly bring a baby into the world, but through their change of attitude they were able to change the course of their past karma, becoming very much happier as a result.

There was a young man who looked very energetic and lively, however he did not seem to really 'see' anything, and when he looked at people he never really saw them. When he came for therapy there were two psychic holes where his eyes should be. During regression he found out that in another lifetime he had had his eyes gouged out, and although his physical eyes were intact they were strangely insensitive to the world around him and he acted like a blind man. This was obviously a psychic injury that had manifested as two white holes. The angels performed psychic surgery on the eyes; drawing them back from the life before they were taken out, psychically reconstructing them, cleansing them and then gently allowing them to become one with the physical eyes. After this had been completed the angels put a special spiritual substance into the eyes to enable him to have a very much wider, as well as deeper, vision.

The awakening of psychic awareness

Far too many people fantasise about becoming psychic, not really taking into consideration all the factors that are involved. One man told me how much he wanted to be clairvoyant, imagining that he would only see angels, fairies, brightly coloured auras and angelic halos. He did not consider for one moment that he would also see the complete

167

reverse if he were to become truly psychic. When I discussed this with him, he changed his mind very quickly, almost recoiling at the very thought of being psychic.

I met a unique woman in Brazil who was able to materialise all the positive aspects of a person's nature, as well as the negative. Either way was a dangerous consideration if the person suffered from even a moderately strong ego. Seeing only the positive aspects of past life experiences could be mentally and emotionally disquieting, causing all sorts of delusions of grandeur and Messiah complexes! Only seeing the negative past could drive a man out of his body with sheer terror or deep remorse regarding his past actions, simply because he would not be able to resist judging his past misdeeds within the context of his present time-consciousness.

Being psychic could be quite a burden without the proper purification and state of awareness to blend with the condition. I once met a psychiatrist from France who was very psychic and he could see spirits as part of his everyday existence. He did not, however, really understand what he saw or why he saw it, because although he was clairvoyantly very open, his heart chakra was closed. This meant that he did not have the ability to comprehend inwardly what he was seeing and did not really know what he could do to help the spirits around him, or how to help himself. Some clairvoyants can be positively dangerous when their heart chakra is not properly opened, as they can perhaps unwittingly give out inaccurate information about someone, which may not be in their best interest.

Often clairvoyance is associated with spiritual development, but this could not be further from the truth. Someone who has been on heavy drugs or has taken large quantities of alcohol could become adversely clairvoyant, at a high price of course. A few people have been known to become clairvoyant after accidents or after a severe illness, but this does not mean that they have suddenly become more spiritual as a result.

The opening of the third eye does not necessarily mean visual clairvoyance, since there are different kinds of clairvoyance that may be more suitable to specific individuals. There is of course the 'seeing' kind of vision, where a person is able to see auras and also see positive and negative beings. It is very unusual for a clairvoyant to have multi-dimensional vision, which means seeing inside, above, beside and beneath an object; also to see the energies within the plants and trees and in human beings, to see spirits and to understand exactly why they are there. This type of clairvoyance is unique, but the vision is usually coloured by the clairvoyant's personal hang-ups, as they do not usually undergo spiritual purification before doing their type of work, so there is always an element of danger in their ability to perceive the inner reality of the person whom they are endeavouring to assist.

There is the clairvoyance of 'feeling' and 'sensing', but the safest form is 'knowing'. If someone 'sees' they can be personally very influenced by their perception. If a person is very religious and sees an angel with a pair of wings, that person may automatically think that it is a positive being, although it may be quite the reverse. Even the famous 16th-century magician, Dr John Dee, was hoodwinked when he saw a negative being masquerading as an angel. It really is safer to 'know' than to 'see', unless one has been through a lot of purification and knows the difference between subjective and objective vision.

Blockages to clairvoyance may not necessarily be in the brow chakra or third eye area, they can be found in any part of the body. If a person very strongly desires clairvoyant vision they can block themselves by their attitude. Emotions that can impede clairvoyant vision are 'fear of the supernatural', 'fear of facing the truth', 'desire for power', and even raw emotions like 'anger' and 'hate'. There is usually a very strong personal karma related to one's inner perception and awareness. We all have the potential to be telepathic as well as clairvoyant, it is the unresolved karmic condition that stops this energy from flowing freely. When a person seriously starts to come to terms with a number of aspects of his or her past karma, clairvoyance in one of its many forms usually starts to unfold if it is right for the person in this particular incarnation.

There is little point in trying to stimulate physically the pituitary and pineal glands (the chakras connected to the inner vision or the psychic centres in the brain related to clairvoyance) until a major part of the negative karma has been initially worked on, and the heart chakra has been purified in order to make it possible for us to even begin to comprehend what we 'see' with humility and gentleness.

There are all kinds of exotic treatments to assist with the awakening of clairvoyant vision, including a special combination of gem remedies to help to improve psychic sensitivity, and colour therapy under the guidance of an experienced practitioner, to help to stimulate the psychic centres in the body, including the third eye.

Water potentised by the amethyst stone creates the vibrational energy of the stone within the water, which can be further energised by the rays of the sun. When used, this promotes healing and stimulation of the psychic faculties. Although one cannot ignore the fact that any negative emotions that impede awareness need to be dealt with first.

All of this without a true understanding of love is virtually meaningless, however. Psychic awareness is greatly enhanced as a result of releasing past negative karma, and the whole process can be helped through the various methods I've mentioned.

Extraterrestrial interference

During my 20 years as a therapist I have come across people from all walks of life who have been affected with negative psychic implants by beings from other planets and solar systems. Members of the media are still expected to keep any serious information they obtain regarding extraterrestrial contacts or flying saucer phenomena a secret, and when the news is finally allowed to be released it is usually several years later. However, a lot of research is being carried out into UFO sightings, abductions, aliens etc, and several books have been written.

A large number of people have been contacted telepathically by extraterrestrials and there have been many flying saucers, as well as corn circles and sightings in different parts of the world. If this information is reported on at all in the press it is usually ridiculed. Many governmental bodies, including those of the USA, UK and Russia all keep a very close check on any sightings, landings, encounters or abductions. For example, hynotherapist and writer, Dolores Cannon, works for MUFON (Mutual UFO Network) helping individuals to acclimatise themselves after extraterrestrial communication or abduction.

Many of the pilots who fly small aircraft over the Nazca plains in Peru have told me that it is not uncommon to see spacecraft. They treat such incidents as just part of their workaday routine. There have been many landings in that area, details of which have been reported to the United Nations. The South American, Sixto Paz, claims to have had many 'encounters of that special kind', having a deep understanding of the basic reasons why extraterrestrials are endeavouring to help humanity to cope with the great changes that are now happening on this planet, sending coded messages through the corn circles and through sensitively attuned individuals who are capable of understanding as well as assimilating aspects of their advanced knowledge and technology.

When I was in Brazil I met two space beings who had taken on human bodies from birth, and were able to share their knowledge and communicate freely without frightening anyone through strange behaviour nor attracting any unnecessary attention by having an unusual body. One of them was in fact a spiritual teacher and spent long periods of time with the extraterrestrials learning how to expand brain power and improve memory retention through special breathing and stretching exercises.

The positive aliens would like to help us to come to terms with some of our global problems, revealing a strong concern for the chaos and confusion that is increasing on our planet through man's mindless desire for self-destruction. The man-in-the-street knows very little about aliens, only what he sees on the television and cinema screens, and whatever is allowed to be printed in the newspapers. This is a great pity as the extraterrestrials would like to make genuine communication with much larger groups of people, without causing unnecessary fear or panic.

Abductions and implants

Unfortunately, there are negative extraterrestrials just as there are positive and negative people, and these negative beings cause disruption through their repeated abductions of human beings against their conscious will for experimental purposes. This puts their positive brothers in

172

a very bad light and as a result there is naturally confusion regarding the motives of all alien visitors from outer space. It seems that positive as well as negative aliens have a lot of sorting out to do between themselves before a freer and more public communication with our positive brothers is really prudent or advisable.

Many varied and different types of implants have been released through Psycho-Regression over the years. It is quite amazing how many different types there are. These can be put into any part of the body or aura, depending on what information is required by the negative alien. Although these implants are not physically solid, they have their own density within the etheric and astral, and can be inwardly recognised by the abductee when in a receptive state of consciousness. All kinds of psychic substances connected with extraterrestrial interference have been released during therapy, including metal discs (in the body or aura), wires in the brain, special stones that are unrecognisable on planet earth, metallic dust and miniature 'radio receivers'. These are some of the objects located and transmuted through the help of the angelic forces. The interesting thing is that many of the same objects have been released from people with totally different backgrounds, cultures and age groups, and from both sexes. These objects are used either to amplify or relay information to a key source of extraterrestrial energy.

When I was in Greece, a woman came to see me advocating strongly that there was nothing wrong with her and I began to wonder what was coming next. She continued to declare that everything was really fine, just as long as she did not read, see or hear anything about flying saucers or extraterrestrials. During the subsequent session of regression we found out that she had been very recently abducted by a group of aliens who were very interested in her psychic sensitivity and her

173

strongly-centred creativity, and they wanted to monitor her activities through planting small metal discs into her aura. These beings were not 'evil' in the traditional 'diabolical sense of the term' in that they were not harbouring a desire to kill, harm or injure. However, they were researching into their own interests at someone else's expense.

According to their own moral code they really thought that their motives were correct, which of course they were not by our moral standards. The woman had been terrified by the experience and during therapy she released 'emotional shock' and 'very deep fear' as a result. She also needed to know why she had inwardly attracted such an unwelcome intrusion into her personal space, thereby discovering the festering deep wounds from the past that had made her exceptionally open and vulnerable to the aliens' influence.

ABDUCTION WITH A POSITIVE OUTCOME

There have also been abductions with a positive outcome.

Brazilian clergyman Herminio Rees was abducted when he and his wife were driving along the highway at night in Brazil. A very large object suddenly appeared in the sky and they were totally amazed by the luminosity emanating from the object. They were not able to identify what it was at the time. Suddenly, and without warning, the car was magnetically drawn up into the spaceship. Herminio must have spent many hours being taught by them, although during this experience he had no concept of time. He was given special breathing exercises to stimulate parts of the brain that generally remain dormant within the average human being and he was also taught how to extend his psychic and spiritual awareness. Soon after this experience, Herminio set up a centre of Transcendental Studies in San

Paulo, Brazil, in order to help people to benefit from this unique form of knowledge. These aliens were understanding and helpful and only wanted to teach humanity to become more aware and balanced.

Negative alien investigation teams are interested in people who are unusual and often those who exhibit paranormal sensitivity, indicating that they have a latent or active potential that can be utilised. Some of the more negative types of aliens, however, are just interested in a straightforward 'takeover', so that they can control the person like a puppet, using him or her to their advantage to promote their own spurious activities. Such 'takeovers' can affect people from all stratas of society, the aliens often going for 'the big fish' so that more people can be subtly influenced. This can only happen if a person allows him or herself to be emotionally tossed around like a boat in the rough seas, for if he or she were to be connected to the God-within, then all of this would seem like fantasy without substance, these negative energies dispersing like puffy clouds.

One needs to have a healthy respect for what is considered to be 'fantasy' in order to maintain a healthy equilibrium. Negative extreterrestrial interference need not come within our sphere of reality, although it can and does happen to people who are not inwardly connected to who and what they really are. When the heart chakra starts to awaken like a flower in the springtime, an inner quickening takes place. As one begins to tread the path of self-knowledge the intuition and primal instincts become quite naturally sharpened, the person feeling much more inwardly connected with his or her Guardian Angel and spiritual helpers. When an inner connection begins to take place, then a natural protection from such negative influences is the inevitable result. However, one needs spiritual vision in order to perceive the genuine as well as the false.

We all need to be in a constant state of learning and discovery, and if this process stops, we rapidly start to age, becoming fixed in our ideas and beliefs. Really there is no resting place for a genuine seeker of the inner reality. The same applies to the heart of Psycho-Regression, as this is also in a constant state of change, and once new discoveries present themselves to me then the information becomes an integral part of the therapy. This has to be inwardly verified with the help of the angels and the divine beings that work with me, in conjunction with my own specialised knowledge gained during many years of research into unusual dimensions of healing.

9

INTEGRATING SUB-PERSONALITIES

The majority of us spend many lives behind one mask or another before we finally start shedding the unwanted present as well as shells of past life masks that clutter up the awareness of the present moment.

A French woman I spoke to during a seminar suddenly came to the astounding realisation that through spiritual purification one gradually sheds one's mask or personality. She looked wide-eyed and quite distraught at the very thought of shedding her personality, and could not imagine how she could successfully survive without her mask. The truth of the matter was that she did not want to shed it and it is still very much with her today. She may want to hold on to her collection of masks for several more incarnations until she finally tires of them, deciding that it is time they were relinquished like the deciduous trees that joyfully shed their leaves each year.

The present-day personality is comprised of many likes and dislikes, pet hates and fears, ideas and fixations that have been accumulated over the centuries. Parental emotions and ideologies also help to shape the outer mask of a developing child, but the problems really start to surface when a person continues to look through his or her parents' eyes as an adult, or becomes emotionally frozen because of an unresolved experience when he or she was still a child.

The positive aspects of all the accumulated experiences of our present and past personalities need to be integrated so that we can enjoy using our maximum potential. If we were a great artist or a farmer, scientist or circus clown in another life, there is no reason why we cannot use these abilities within our present existence, even if the energies manifest differently within our new personality. In Chapter 10, I will explain how it is possible to connect with your primal powers, some of which have already been strongly developed through previous personalities. However, this can only be safely achieved once a person has undergone a very comprehensive purification programme. We are now going to find out about deeper layers of our past personalities, and how we can get to know and successfully integrate them so that they do not create an inner turbulence with which we are unable to cope.

If you invited all of your past personalities to a party, it would be like trying to mix together a concoction of oil and water. Many of the personalities would not get on as they would have nothing in common; some would remain detached and disinterested; some might try to make an impression; and several may be obnoxious or violent. At a social gathering or party, a good host or hostess invites guests who are likely to mix and not people who are hostile, ravishing, robbing or creating a disturbance with each other. It would take a very unusual robber to befriend a princess and not to rob her of her jewels, or a nun to accept a prostitute wholeheartedly, a murderer really to sit and listen to what a spiritual teacher has to share, a Sumo wrestler to talk lightheartedly to a starving and impoverished woman, or a lustful, drunken man to talk intelligently and with sensitivity to a shy young girl. If these personalities got together, of course, the party would be a disaster; only an outsider might see the funny side and even then the outsider would need to be emotionally detached to understand what he or she saw with compassion and humour.

It is necessary for us to make friends with all of the sub-personalities which lie beneath the surface of our consciousness. We need to understand who they are, what we have learnt through their past experiences and how they came to be part of us. Every personality has positive characteristics that we can assimilate and integrate. We also need to confront openly the negative aspects of these personalities, being ready to understand how in the past they came to follow the line of least resistance, perhaps through living their lives selfishly or dangerously. When we approach the negative traits of our sub-personalities, we begin gradually to accept ourselves as we have ceased judging. We learn to stop crucifying ourselves with inaccurate ideas about who we really are, or overloading ourselves with past guilt and only then do we start to become an easier person to be with and also a lot more human. There are many people who do not judge themselves harshly, harbouring little recrimination or guilt connected with their actions from the past. However, there is a great deal of difference between the person who indiscriminately accepts him or herself, and the person who understands his or her inherent weakness without recrimination, but knowing that change is needed.

There are individuals who really do not think that they need to alter anything; if this is what they feel they should therefore follow their instincts and hope that they are correct. Such a person may find him or herself at a spiritual crossroads, several hundred or thousand years later in his or her own uniquely individual process of spiritual unfoldment. Everyone's journey is different, with some people appearing to be slow at assimilating their experiences for a number of lives, who then may suddenly accelerate their learning process, spiritually going forward in leaps and bounds. It is really not possible to judge anyone in terms of 'spiritual advancement', as many of us still have a full-blown party going on beneath the surface of our conscious awareness, our feeling of well-being and wholeness being greatly affected by how well our internal guests are relating. Though we are the creator of the peace or confusion within us, we are by no means aware of the sources of our external reactions and attitudes of the different personalities as they relate to the world at large when they are stimulated into activity.

A sub-personality may lie dormant for many years, only surfacing when a corresponding situation presses the button of its emergence into consciousness. Many sub-personalities can be comparatively superficial, where a person has had numerous lives in order to learn specific lessons. This superficial layer is known as **Layer 1** or the outer layer of the sub-personality spectrum.

Layer 2 incorporates the range of the *great* or *notorious* past personalities. A person can often manifest a very strong creative aspect with one of his or her personalities, which can be anything from a self-deluded martyr to the genius of Leonardo da Vinci. These great or notorious personalities can often still remain emotional victims, although continuing to be creative in their sphere.

In **Layer 3** are the deeply submerged and disowned personalities, and are often the ones that we do not wish consciously to remember. Those in this layer

180

are usually connected with past 'aggressor person-alities'.

These sub-personalities are divided up into three layers, in order to demonstrate the types of conditions that can occur as these personalities surface. There are doubtless many more possible sub-divisions, but for the purposes of this book we can keep to three headings.

LAYER 1

Layer 1 is found just below the surface of the mask of the present-day personality. Some people are very naïve about the idea of the number of lives we all lead; even if they can imagine more than one, then they can only imagine half a dozen at the most! In fact we usually live countless lives, so there are a lot of unintegrated aspects of past personalities that are within us, waiting for our attention. It seems that in a particular incarnation a specific set of personalities become more pronounced, probably depending on the purpose of our life in this particular existence. As the more superficial personalities gradually become more integrated through understanding and self-acceptance, then the deeper ones are able to emerge safely, allowing room for the disowned personalities to at least make their presence known.

The personalities in Layer 1 are fairly acceptable to a person undergoing regression, as they are usually personalities who have gone through considerable hardship with their soul's decision to learn a particular lesson.

Often the inner decision to incarnate is connected with deeply-buried guilt associated with a strong desire for self-punishment connected with the submerged personalities inhabiting Layer 3. As we are all our own judge, jury and executioner, we really punish ourselves life after life, until we finally get it right by changing our attitude. It is important to understand that no personality or 'mask' wants to change; it is very happy to stay just the way it is, continuing to perpetuate its habitual existence like some stoic old ghost that persists in haunting the same piece of ground century after century.

For example, the personality of the *peasant* thinks and acts like a peasant, not imagining being able to have anything more than a peasant would have. The negative side of this personality could be connected with low self-esteem, limited thinking and limited expectations. The positive aspect could be appreciation of the simple things in life, like love of nature, earthiness and so much more.

The negative side of a cloistered *nun* or *priest* could be fear of life and sexuality, emotional withdrawal, separation between what is considered to be spiritual and physical, rigidity or fear of freedom. The positive aspects of a nun or priest could be the love of God, meditation, prayer, the ability to be alone, strength, solidarity and humility.

The negative personality of a *nomad* could manifest fear of restriction and responsibility and perhaps a fear of enclosed spaces. The positive aspect is love of nature and open spaces, and love of adventure and freedom.

The negative side of the personality of a clown may manifest as low self-esteem, desire for humiliation, loneliness, hypersensitivity to the feelings of others, with the positive aspects manifesting perhaps as desire for fun and laughter, and to make others happy, joy of humour and of life itself.

The negative side of the personality of the *knight* who apparently fights for might and right, could be arrogance, pride and self-deception, with the positive aspects manifesting as selflessness, kindness, thoughtfulness, courage and strength.

The above are just a few examples of Layer 1 that could emerge. All of these personalities are quite acceptable, even if they were somewhat misguided in that particular lifetime. Usually the personalities have become out of balance due to past misunderstandings or lack of awareness, the peasant perhaps being too simple-minded and willingly taking on the role of the 'victim'. And the personality of the priest could affect the way a person is now, like his sexuality in present time, especially if he has not released his past vows of celibacy, chastity and obedience! The knight errant could be over-enthusiastic about 'the spiritual path', easily getting lost along the way, because he was so sure that this could not happen to him, only to others.

There are also other personalities to be found in Layer 1, including people who have suddenly died in a war or disaster in a recent lifetime and have returned quite quickly. The auric bodies of these types of personalities have not had time to settle into the new psychic genetic imprint between lives, so the injuries are carried close to the surface of the new personality. This means that the host personality can suffer as a result by feeling unusual aches and pains which are usually medically diagnosed as psychosomatic, yet can actually be conditions connected to the recent disaster from another lifetime.

The spirits of stillborn and aborted babies can also reside in Layer 1, as if psychically fossilised, often working out karma from previous past life experiences, perhaps learning to appreciate the sacred nature of life or helping others to understand the same.

It is very unusual indeed for Layer 1 to have any 'aggressor personalities'. The victim personalities are the ones that surface the most. These are comprised of people who have been poor, persecuted or have had a very difficult time, either dying too young, or in traumatic circumstances. There is no such thing as a completely 'innocent victim', as there is always an inner reason for magnetically attracting adverse circumstances.

When a man finds himself at the foot of the gallows for a crime that he has not committed, we must ask why. Reincarnation offers a logical answer, for he could be inwardly reconnecting with a chain of events which he may have put into motion many incarnations before. When you think of the billions of people on earth, you cannot help but wonder why some people seem to suffer in extraordinary ways whereas others seem to live comparatively happy lives.

Jung would probably call such events 'meaningful coincidence', implying that there is an inner factor operating, that magnetically brings unresolved conditions together. If one looks beyond the realms of chance or blind coincidence, one cannot but wonder why a murderer should be attracted to a particular person out of millions. Through an understanding of the karmic law of cause and effect, one cannot help wondering how well-acquainted the victim and the murderer may have been in previous existences and what transpired then, in order to bring about such a devastating present-day effect.

Our mind is only consciously aware of this life's experience. However, our inner being is part of our karmic past and this is the reality from which the law of cause and effect operates. We cannot overlook or avoid who and what we are and the need to integrate every aspect of ourselves in order to find inner wholeness and harmony.

LAYER 2

There can be similar types of personalities residing within the middle layer of the psyche, although they seem to live more intensely, passionately and creatively, generally being more strongly developed characters.

Although the personalities in Layer 2 have a lot more potential, they can also harbour a lot more pain, resentment, anger, jealousy and revenge. Usually the host personality pushes these more dynamic personalities deeper into the middle of the psyche as a measure of self-protection against feeling any of the backlash of their stronger emotions that have been perhaps unexpressed within this particular lifetime. This means that the personalities that inhabit the middle layer of the psyche can be a lot more volatile when stirred into action through similar circumstances encountered in the life of the host personality.

One young woman became very emotionally disturbed every time she heard the Last Post played on Armistice Sunday, partially going into spontaneous regression and remembering when she was killed as a soldier in the First World War. In this case the bugle acted as a trigger to this usually dormant personality.

Another unusual case of a Layer 2 personality was a woman who was a highly respected cardinal in Italy in another life, and she found it very difficult to connect with religion or God in her present existence. During regression she found out that she had taken advantage of an innocent young girl, leaving her pregnant as a result. The cardinal was never found out, but had to live with himself on a day-to-day basis, his guilt gradually consuming his outwardly successful existence. He lost his self-respect and neglected his appearance, becoming dirty and dishevelled, and feeling that God could only punish him for what he felt to be such wickedness. Many years later he died of despair, and with a feeling of guilt that he was never able to confess openly. After he had left his body his spirit realised that he had not been true to himself and he was filled with remorse, self-hatred and guilt. After releasing these past emotions the host personality received absolution, thereby gaining a deep and fulfilling connection with God. The woman became a lot happier in her present life, and for the first time she was able to pray without feeling inwardly damned.

The negative aspects of the personalities in Layer 2 can be activated when stimulated by present time circumstances. Being too easily affected by personal unresolved desires and unfulfilled longings, and not seeing things in the right perspective, can create havoc within the consciousness of the host personality.

LAYER 3

This layer comprises disowned and deeply submerged personalities which the person either does not want to remember or cannot cope with at his or her present stage of evolution. Personalities that inhabit this level of inner space can be either saints or sinners, or even connected with lives lived on other planets, which is not as uncommon as one might at first suppose.

The 'aggressor' personalities are generally in Layer 3, as they are part of the consciously disowned variety. From a negative standpoint, these personalities often carry with them deeply buried guilt which may be connected with the misuse of power, including black magic, violence and cruelty. From a therapeutic standpoint you know that you are touching the depths of the psyche when these aggressor personalities begin to surface, as they are so heavily camouflaged by the victim and the neutral personalities of Layers 1 and 2. It seems that victims act as decoys for the aggressors, as well as the other types of personalities that one may be unable to confront until the time is right. It would be dangerous to force an aggressor personality up to the surface of consciousness before the smaller fry had first been dealt with.

If the aggressor is strong enough it could take control over a number of weaker or neutral types of personalities. If it is unusually strong-willed and had the back-up of the powers of darkness, including past black magic connections, then it could usurp the position of the host personality. And when this type of takeover occurs with a foul-mouthed, uncouth type of person, then the person is generally labelled 'mad'. However, if a deeply submerged personality happens to be cunning, devious and negatively charming (like Count Dracula for example), and takes over the host personality, then no one may be any the wiser regarding this takeover if both of the personalities complement one another. It would be very naïve of us to think that these personalities are unable to take over weak host personalities when psychiatric units and prisons are full of people who have been controlled by the more uncouth, unreconciled spirits of the past.

A person can wallow in self-pity if they have had a particularly difficult life, without taking into consideration the cause of the pattern of the stream of victim personalities.

There is an interesting illustration of this concerning a young man who felt that his father did not really love him. The father was not a particularly kind or loving man, especially to his son. During regression the young man was regressed into another life when he was a knight. He ran a commoner through with his sword because he did not happen to agree with what he had said; he found out that this man was his present-time father. In another incarnation as a male sheikh he lived in a large house with a number of servants and several wives. One day an important silk trader came to stay with him as his special house guest, and as a token of his great esteem for this man, he gave away one of his wives who loved him the most. This wife was also his present-day father. In his present life he had problems communicating with his emotionally cold father because of these unresolved past-life situations of once running him through with a sword, and in another life giving him away! After being regressed he understood all too well the root cause of his communication problems, ceasing to place the blame on anyone else's shoulders. He continued to integrate the more ruthless aspects of himself that revealed themselves within the deeper levels of his psyche.

Very powerful positive personalities also reside within Layer 3, remaining concealed for very good reasons. If the host personality becomes prematurely aware of their presence, attempting to force it to the surface, they may develop a large ego problem if they were not very inwardly balanced or had not undergone any form of therapy.

There are many people in spiritual circles who imagine that they were someone very important in a past life, being at least a Joan of Arc or St Francis of Assisi, or some great philosopher or mystic, rejecting any personality from humbler origins. One needs to experience the full length of the spectrum from beggar to Buddha, in order to find an inner state of peace and balance, where no judgement exists.

There are a number of people who have personalities connected with other planetary systems. A Swedish woman spent all of her savings, as well as borrowing extra money to travel around the world. She did not realise it at the time, but she was unconsciously looking for her spiritual mate whom she had originally met on another planet. During regression she found that she had a totally different type of body with four legs and a long neck, as did the one she loved. She experienced great joy at making such a wonderful connection again, even though it was through regression.

Several months later they met 'in the flesh', both delighted to discover that they were both in human bodies, of the opposite sex, inwardly feeling that they had known each other for centuries (which of course they had). They were attracted to one another just as strongly and became close again in human form. They later did further regression and found out that they were very strongly connected spiritually and were meant to live and to work together in this particular lifetime in order to make up for many lives which they had spent apart.

An American woman underwent a great deal of therapy, working on Layers 1 and 2 of the sub-personalities, and no one could have been more surprised than her when she discovered during regression that she was a woman living at the time of Christ, also finding out that she knew him personally. She was even more amazed to find herself anointing his feet with her long hair, and then realised that she had been Mary Magdalene.

When a very strong positive or negative sub-personality emerges during regression, the intellectual mind occasionally impinges on the validity of the experience, especially after centuries of conditioning in the belief that the logical mind is superior to the intuitive. Further information regarding the experience then starts to emerge, together with the in-depth emotion connected with the emergent personality. One would have to be a first-class Hollywood script writer, as well as a star actor or actress with excess money and time to waste, in order to make up and recount what takes place during Psycho-Regression.

When a disowned personality surfaces, a person can take time to integrate the positive aspects within the

189

psyche, although he or she releases the negative aspects during the process of Psycho-Regression.

Quite unexpectedly during a session of regression, a man realised that he was a practitioner of the black arts in Atlantis and stole people's life force in the way that one drinks fruit juice through a straw! He realised without a doubt that this had happened and the session moved him to depths of grief beyond tears. During the therapy he understood the reasons why he had sunk to such depths, the desire for power being even more important than individual life. He released all of the negative emotions within the sub-personality of the black arts magician, finding out that his positive qualities were strength, power, energy and vision, which were enhanced through the therapy in order that this personality could redirect his power in the service of God.

However it still took him quite a time to readjust to his new energy, utilising it positively within his everyday life, as well as accepting the fact that whatever his conscience was in Atlantis, it was obviously very different to what it is now in present time, acceptance of the past being a very important part of an effective integration.

Sub-personalities and possession

It is not uncommon for a person to be taken over by a number of sub-personalities that control the host personality, as in the famous classic story of *The Three Faces of Eve* by C.H. Thighten. You may also have seen the film which starred Joanne Woodward. We all have sub-personalities but they do not usually surface without assistance, unless there is some strong external stimuli to bring them to consciousness.

People who strongly identify with their sub-personalities are not always initially possessed by them. When a person becomes too engrossed with the past, they can then over-identify with their past feelings and ideas, eventually getting taken over by the personality. Especially if a person's present life is not very eventful, then it is not uncommon for a person to fantasise about some past glory.

Many years ago when I was on holiday visiting Sorrento, I got involved in conversation with a hotelier who owned a beautiful hotel overlooking the sea. He seemed to be a quiet, intelligent and pleasant man. During a lighthearted conversation about the beauty and magic of Sorrento, he suddenly mentioned his interest in the 16th-century Italian poet Tasso. When I showed an interest in poetry he invited me to dine with him that very evening in order to tell me all about his favourite poet. We sat at an eight-foot wooden table, with red candles placed at each end. After spending two hours talking non-stop over dinner, he offered to show me Tasso's relics and, without waiting for a reply, he showed me several pairs of glasses that had been worn by the poet, a few of his teeth which he had managed to obtain through relatives, also clothes and several books that Tasso had owned. I was young, a little too polite, and did not have the opportunity to say very much, but I was inwardly very interested in what or who possessed this man to go to what I thought even then were great lengths to preserve his memory.

At that moment I had some idea of what was to follow, and sure enough this man then offered to show me an exact replica of the room that Tasso had lived in. In sheer disbelief I agreed to see it and he opened a large trapdoor revealing some steps leading into a lower chamber down which we both proceeded to walk. We were suddenly in a large room with a wax figure of Tasso sitting at the desk surrounded

191

by books, papers and elegant 16th-century furniture. I was amazed and in the process of thinking that it was all rather a pointless exercise, when he opened yet another door in the floor, revealing another room below. At this stage I could not believe that there was anything else to see, but the secret room told me differently. This was a replica of a prison cell, with a lifelike wax figure of the poet Tasso lying dying and bleeding on a roughly-made bed, with a ball and chain around one of his ankles. I felt a very unpleasant atmosphere in that room, as though this hotelier had perhaps unconsciously trapped the spirit of the dead poet within the prison of his own mind. By the time we returned up the steps, I felt really ready to go; then just as I was about to leave the hotel, two American ladies turned up to see the man who looked very pleased to see them and asked if they would like to see some of the relics of the poet Tasso! . . .

This was an advanced case of possession of a sub-personality, where the man was living the life of another person, almost to the exclusion of his present life, and one can only surmise that he had almost been taken over by another personality.

There are, however, far less obvious cases of sub-personality possession. For example, during my years as a therapist and a healer I have met many men and women who strongly identify with lives connected to witchcraft, especially during the Middle Ages. Some of them just feel inwardly that they were burnt or tortured for practising witchcraft, and when they were regressed this was found to be true. Some people more strongly identify with these personalities and change their mode of dress as a result, wearing black or the modern equivalent in fashion to the Middle Age period in history, sometimes extravagantly wearing rings on every finger. I have come across many ex-witches, but have probably encountered only comparatively few inquisitors residing within the depth of Layer 3 of the psyche.

I met an Australian man who was extremely psychic but emotionally unbalanced; he strongly identified with Cardinal Richelieu, the 17th-century French cardinal and statesman, who was the prime minister of Louis XIII, wearing similar clothes and regalia, and acting in a regal manner which he could not afford to emulate. He had no desire to change his inner state, as he really did not think that there was anything wrong to be put right.

There was a Scotsman who was said to have been the reincarnation of William Shakespeare, and he was able to recite from memory many of his plays, incorporating all the characters simultaneously and very eloquently. He appeared to want to keep this identity a secret, although everyone with whom he came into contact seemed to learn very quickly about his claimed past identity, but he never disclosed the truth about his feelings as he did not desire or even want to find out more about his life as Shakespeare. One would have thought that he would have displayed a little healthy curiosity concerning his deeper feelings about such an important matter. He was a very interesting and brilliant man, but was not interested in regression therapy, his insights concerning Shakespeare surfacing quite naturally in his everyday life. He obviously managed to handle this particular aspect of his nature adequately.

When a person claims to have been a famous historical or religious past personality like Florence Nightingale, Beethoven or St Francis of Assisi, a person usually encounters far more scepticism and disbelief than they would if they stated that they have been someone infamous like Machiavelli, Lucrezia Borgia, Salome or Adolf Hitler. Such claimants would probably be treated with dry humour or may merely be considered eccentric. However, when a person claims to have been a famous and positive past personality, they may be outrageously ridiculed, thought to be a meglomaniac, or even plain mad.

It is understandable that such people are treated in this way, as the cause of the condition is not usually understood and is therefore judged accordingly. I have met several women claiming to be the reincarnation of the Virgin Mary, also Jesus Christ, Shakespeare, Paracelsus, Cardinal Richelieu, Madame Blavatsky, and several men claiming to be the notorious magician Aleister Crowley! Only one claimant can be correct and alive at the one time. The others are identifying with a popular model, perhaps because it bears a remarkable resemblance to a similar personality within the claimant from another lifetime which they are strongly identifying with because of unresolved experiences connected with their past.

Many years ago I met a man with several strong (Layer 3) sub-personalities all struggling for supremacy. On the several occasions that I met him in conjunction with my work, I never knew which personality was going to turn up at my door. One day he stood at the door unsmiling, dressed as an Egyptian pharoah, another time he opened the door quite differently, with a smile and dressed as a Jewish rabbi, and yet another time he nonchantly appeared immaculately dressed in a dinner jacket with a black bow tie. His wife was mainly controlled by one past personality. She lived, breathed and acted like an Egyptian priestess, but politely tolerated what she considered to be her husband's occasional relapses from his true pharoah personality to the lesser personalities of the rabbi and the lord of the manor. They ran what they considered to be a spiritual school for initiates on the path of enlightenment and they considered themselves to be very advanced spiritual teachers. What they did not realise was that when the positive side of one's nature becomes amplified through spiritual practices, then the negative also surfaces and has to be acknowledged, as well as carefully dealt with. This man and woman ignored such obvious dangers and their divided personalities became more fragmented over the years, allowing a satanic entity to take possession over all of their personalities, and cunningly leading them to believe that they were becoming more powerful and exalted. Even then they did not think that anything unusual had occurred as their pride had led them in the wrong direction. This is an example of how things can be altered in the present life, if people are not willing to face the negative aspects of themselves.

Criminals, such as murderers, thieves, rapists and sadists are often sporadically possessed by negative sub-personalities because of a number of inherent weaknesses in the host personality. If we have a spiritual debit account that continues to increase through lack of goodwill, then we are going to have to pay the debt in order to avoid spiritual bankruptcy. The criminal personality is not willing to pay his debts so they are forced upon that person in a very physical way by being put into prison. This really does not solve the problem, but it only keeps the situation under a very superficial control until the person is perhaps released for good behaviour. Then the sub-personality can eventually re-emerge in order to perpetuate its particular pattern of anti-social behaviour. I am not suggesting that all criminals react in this way, as that would be too simplistic, although I am saying that a large percentage of criminals are possessed by one or several sub-personalities and unresolved karma connected with this as well as other lifetimes.

Dr Kenneth Walker in his book *Diagnosis of Man*, stated

that the criminal personality usually has a severely unbalanced endocrine system, including pituitary and pineal malfunctions. I would also add that this is symptomatic of something very much deeper, indicating in many instances severe sub-personality possession problems, as well as possession by external spirits and demons. After a murderer has been caught, how many times have you heard the phrase 'I don't know what happened, I was beside myself', and doubtless the person was, as probably another personality had taken over. Another truism is 'I don't know what came over me.' One does wonder! I agree that the criminal is by no means always 100 per cent aware of what he or she is doing when committing a crime, the anger, hate or jealousy creating a temporary aberration of consciousness, allowing one or more malevolent sub-personalities to surface and take control. People like Jack the Ripper, Myra Hindley and Charles Manson probably had a number of very heavy Layer 3 personalities that surfaced when provoked by the right circumstances. The classic story of Dr Jekyll and Mr Hyde, written by Robert L. Stevenson in 1886, graphically illustrates the battle between the positive and the negative personalities within one man, Dr Jekyll. Dr Jekyll's medical experimentation to transform himself with the use of potions, created the personification of his own evil, Mr Hyde, this unredeemed part of his nature only surfacing when deliberately provoked by Dr Jekyll. Insidiously Hyde takes control, attempting to destroy Jekyll entirely. As Dr Jekyll, he is very aware of the evil personality of Hyde residing within him and is horrified by the repercussions brought about by this manifestation of his own evil. He feels that the situation can only be overcome through his own death.

This story is a very dramatic illustration of the struggle that can take place within each one of us.

Even if it happens to be on a milder scale it is no less real. The criminals of this world need a lot more care and attention given to the primal causes of their problems.

It is often naïvely thought that penal punishment will stop the majority of criminals from returning to prison. Criminals need to be understood in a new way and not simply punished for past misdemeanours. This does not really get to the core of the problem. There is some good work being done by aware people connected to the government in various parts of the world, usually under the heading of counselling or psychotherapy, though problems connected with reincarnation, spirit possession, or sub-personality disorders are usually controlled with drugs, as this area is generally still not treated on more sensitive therapeutic lines or understood from a psychic or paranormal viewpoint.

A person who has committed a crime could very well have a possessing spirit or sub-personality which may have been lying dormant for many years, the negative side of the person only surfacing under personally emotive situations. If these negative personalities are restricted by confinement and they wish to continue their particular habit patterns, they will go to great lengths to give the world the impression of normality as society sees it, even faking religious conversion.

Convicted rapists, after many years of confinement and behaving like model prisoners, may commit another sexual crime within hours of release. Under confinement where there are no women, there is no stimulus. If the media put as much attention on to the average criminal as they do for sexual criminals perhaps the whole scenario would change. If a weed is not totally removed from the soil, it simply regrows and if the primal cause is not dealt with then the problem re-occurs in one form or another.

People in confinement could benefit from Psycho-

Regression therapy, provided that they have a deep desire for change. Usually when a person has committed a crime there is a chronic psychic overload of unresolved energy within the psyche that needs to be treated. The energy needs to be transmuted gradually over a period of time, as a very predominant negative type of sub-personality would doubtless affect a number of organs as well as other parts of the body, for example various parts of the brain, brow, endocrine system and heart.

We can be positively or negatively affected by our sub-personalities and we all have our self-created prisons to walk freely away from in order for us to find the God-within. This can only be successfully achieved when we have a burning desire to change, and the will to pursue this *system of healing and personal growth*.

10

CONNECTING WITH YOUR PRIMAL POWERS

Since the beginning of recorded history there have been countless allusions to the divinity within man. In a biblical reference (John 10) Jesus Christ openly states 'Ye are Gods', and 'The Father is in me and I in him', inferring that it is really up to us to accept or reject this. I have discussed this with several orthodox Christian clergy who usually skirt round the issue by saying that Christ did not really mean that, he meant that man is a 'bit of God', a 'part of God' or a 'spark of God'. The statement 'Ye are Gods' cannot really be argued about, it just needs to be inwardly absorbed and meditated upon.

The esoteric teachings within all religions encourage a person to connect with the God within or to seek the inner state of Enlightenment, therefore not encouraging external reliance on any person, object or doctrine. The esoteric side of religion can be positively or negative applied, the prayers, meditations or sacramental aspects helping to form a solid foundation to foster the growth of the community, as well as promoting the spiritual awareness within the individual. However, religion is negative when the dogma becomes more important than the essence, leading many to believe truly that their way is the only way to God.

Civilisation brings with it many environmental as well as personal hazards, which can have a detrimental effect on an individual's physical, emotional and spiritual growth. We are surrounded by many effects of an artificially created environment that is gradually destroying this planet. The concrete on the ground that inhibits the life force from the earth, the noise and pollution, including radio activity and artificial preservatives, these are just a few of the hazards we encounter on a daily basis. Our bodies, minds and emotions have to work through these effects and conditions in order even to begin to find the beginnings of sacredness.

Personal purification

Besides releasing past negative karma and sorting out our childhood traumas from this life, we are also inwardly merging and integrating the positive aspects of our past personalities that enhance our creativity and power within our everyday lives. If, for example, you were a knight in another incarnation, the positive attributes of that personality may be strength, endurance and tenacity. These characteristics are enhanced within the person's nature once the negative energies have been released. This naturally applies to all different types of personalities from past existences. If you had been a dogmatic and emotionally rigid type of person, with very fixed ideas about life and sexuality, as these negative traits are released you may discover a loving, warm-hearted and sexually responsive man or woman struggling to get out. He or she could really begin to enjoy life instead of just living it.

When parts of our past personalities are trapped in other time zones we do not really connect with the here and now and we miss out on the simple joy of living truly in the moment, taking full advantage of being in our present time bodies and enjoying every minute of it.

We also need to create a solid foundation for our spiritual activities in order to at least function reasonably harmoniously within our physical world. Many people have been through much spiritual purification in their lifetimes, including meditation, prayer and forms of counselling, and different therapies which include regression and various forms of healing and shamanistic practices. However, I have met a number of trance mediums, psychics and healers who are frequently physically unwell because they do not look after their physical bodies properly, relying too heavily on their spiritual powers and taking their physical vehicles for granted in the process. They do not realise that the body can be likened to an electrical plug, which, if it were to be faulty and a powerful current were to pass through it, then it could blow a fuse.

Personal cleansing and purification of the physical body can be achieved in many ways. There are, however, several essential building blocks to help us to create the foundations of our physical temple.

Detoxification of the physical body is naturally of paramount importance. This can be achieved through carefully selected natural remedies including herbs, homoeopathy or Indian Ayurvedic medicines.

It is also possible to eliminate toxicity through monitored fasting or by following a suitable detoxifying diet like the macrobiotic, fruitarian or the Hay System. The cardinal rule of the Hay System is not to mix carbohydrates with proteins and acid fruits. (See Further Reading: *Food Combining for Health*.)

When food combinations are not properly regulated in a vegetarian diet, a person can suffer from iron deficiency, hypoglycaemia, indigestion and high cholesterol levels, especially if a lot of fried foods and dairy products are eaten. It is vital for people to receive sound advice from trained experts in this field.

Some of the Gurudas gem remedies (see Further Reading) and Bach flower remedies can also help the body's process of elimination. Gem and flower remedies can help people to come to terms with their mental and emotional problems, which in turn can heal the physical body. Australian flower essences also help the eliminatory process on all levels, and when used in conjunction with Psycho-Regression therapy the process can be speeded up considerably.

Another very important part of the purification process which should not be overlooked is the checking and treatment of parasites, worms or fungi. The popular idea is that only children get worms, but this could not be further from the truth as infestation can and does happen at any age.

When I was in the United States I observed the remarkable work of Dr Bob Ramirez, MD and I spent many hours with him when he treated people in his busy Los Angeles practice. Dr Bob, as he was generally called, was also a parasitologist as well as a unique medical doctor. People went to him for many different types of problems including schizophrenia, severe depression, fatigue, chronic anger, sleeplessness and hyperactivity. He also practised radionics and often checked with his pendulum to see if a person was suffering from infestation by any type of parasites, worms or fungi. In a high percentage of cases he found that people did have worms or parasites so he then gave them special herbal remedies in order that they could eliminate the various types of parasites and eggs from the system.

202

In Europe a very inadequate worm remedy is often used to cover a very wide spectrum of worms, parasites (including tropical ones) and fungi. When there are so many different types of parasites a general treatment certainly does not guarantee an effective cure of the problem. The treatment of parasites should at least become a fundamental part of the cleansing process within the orthodox medical field, as well as the alternative medical field, as it is a very vital part of physical purification.

During Dr Bob's many years of researching in this area, he found that when a person with schizophrenia or depression was treated for worms they began to feel a great deal better within weeks, no matter what their original symptoms were. Although he worked on a very physical level, he treated the primal condition medically as well as the parasites.

I talked to many of his patients about their reactions during the course of treatment and I obtained proof of their good results. I also saw many samples of parasites of all shapes and sizes that had been eliminated through the faeces by people of all ages and from all walks of life. Dr Bob got such effective results that people went to visit him from all over the USA. Unfortunately, he died, probably as a result of overwork, and there are not enough suitable people to follow his unusual methods.

It is important to include information like this in my book, as some people might lead themselves into imagining that they are possessed by an evil spirit when they grind their teeth at night, or by a sub-personality when they are very depressed, or by a demon of anxiety when they bite their nails. It may just be that a parasite is the major cause of the problem.

In ancient shamanistic methods of healing, the source of the problem is initially worked on from within outwards and not the reverse. When we work on our mental and emotional problems, we also purify our physical bodies to some extent. It would be unwise to imagine that if we purify our minds and emotions that the physical body will automatically be healed; we are living in a very polluted environment so this would be rather a lot to expect. People often treat their cars with a lot more respect than they do their bodies, though people are now becoming more interested in maintaining their health than they were 10 years ago. Although people have become more health conscious in some respects with diet and exercise, many still do not cleanse or detoxify their bodies on a regular basis. When this is taken seriously and the purification process on all levels, including the physical, has been successfully accomplished, then we are able safely to receive the fruits of our labours through connecting with the primal source of our inner powers with the help of Psycho-Regression.

Primal powers

The majority of people living on earth desire power in one form or another, but how it manifests depends very much upon the spiritual maturity and understanding of the person concerned. A young soul without an inwardly developed sense of widsom may desire power in order to attract attention through some form of adulation, perhaps desiring good looks, wealth or material possessions. A more experienced soul who has incarnated for a longer period of time, learning through his past life experiences, may still desire power, though it may be a great deal more subtle, appearing to be almost non-existent to the undiscerning eye. Desire for power can be camouflaged in many ways, perhaps behind a saintly exterior manifesting a larger than life ultruism or perhaps by a student of enlightenment desiring power in order to feel personally important for their own personal reasons and making secret of it, like some of our politicians, statesmen and churchmen; the public rarely benefiting from this type of inverted egoism.

It would be a very unique person whose motive was as 'pure as the driven snow' when desiring to make contact with the source of his or her primal powers. However, the personal purification programme that includes the cleansing of the mind, emotions and psychic conditions, as well as the physical body, gradually prepares the ground for a safe and effective connection with the spiritual roots of one's very existence. Without going through the initial purification, this would be a dangerous procedure, like building a gold palace in an earthquake zone. The necessity for purification cannot be overstressed as we need to cope with all of the complexities within the human psyche that are affected by past and present-day karma.

After the different types of negative energies have been transmuted and the body has been cleansed, the person is then in a fit state to discover the casket containing many kinds of glittering jewels lying deep within the psyche, longing to be discovered and used creatively according to their individual properties. We are all a veritable power-house, and it is up to each one of us to uncover the different types of power that lie dormant within the deepest levels of our being. We may gradually acquire these powers from many past lifetimes as a result of positively and perhaps selflessly directing our energies in the service of others.

We all have a Guardian Angel, as well as one or more spirit guides, depending upon the type of work that we do in our present life. If someone is involved in making money solely for personal gain and is therefore not using his or her powers creatively, there may be only one or two guides endeavouring to help that person to expand his or her level of perception. If one is actively helping others through the arts or sciences, or is even loosely involved in the service of humanity, then a greater number of guides with different abilities are attracted to help fulfil the task more effectively. Some healers have as many as half a dozen or more major angels, as well as their Guardian Angel, to help them with their work, and also the minor angels which strengthen the different organs within the body.

Many clairvoyants tend to see spirit guides in a similar vein, which could possibly be a result of their own personal projections. Usually American Indians, nuns, monks and Chinese philosophers seem to surface with unfailing regularity. Psychics generally do not see guides as sailors, barrow boys, barmaids, exquisitely beautiful women or weightlifters their choice appearing to be very conventional. This does not mean that the guides which the psychics see are not genuine, though their vision may inhibit the natural enthusiasm of some of the other willing helpers in the spirit world, who do not happen to fall into one of these former categories. It seems very funny that such an attitude prevails with people who claim 'to see'. If you happen to have a motor mechanic or barrow boy as a guide, instead of a monk or philosopher, do not be judgemental, as they are equally caring and compassionate, and doubtless make excellent helpers, often with a very lively and down-to-earth sense of humour.

Many people wonder if spirit guides are an integral part of a person's own primal power or if they are totally separate entities in their own right that give their help when required. The answer is 'yes' to both questions. Many of the spirit guides can be the spiritual counterpart of past personalities which have evolved to such a high degree that they are actively able to assist in the evolutionary process of the incarnated person, whereas other guides tend to come and go, depending upon the person's earthly circumstances.

If, for example, a person is a farmer, he may have specific guides to help him to communicate more easily with nature, but if he decides to become a public speaker and gives up farming then the guides which helped him to connect with the plants and trees may leave him, and different guides connected with communication and oratory may come along to assist him with his work. One man who became a healer rather late in life acquired a band of about 15 guides to assist him with the healing, and when he retired many of these same guides left and only his personal guides remained. Several years later he decided to write a book on healing and a few special guides connected to inspiration and communication came to assist him with the project.

We are referring to two types of spirit guides; those which are a spiritual extension of the person, and the others which temporarily assist when the occasion requires it.

DIFFERENT TYPES OF PRIMAL POWERS

There are many other different types of positive powers that reside deep within the psyche besides spirit guides and angels. These powers manifest themselves in many different ways, taking on the form that is appropriate to the cultural and religious background of the person concerned. The powers can manifest as animals, birds, insects or reptiles, as illustrated in Egyptian and American Indian religious and shamanistic pantheons, where there are many animal-headed gods, golden serpents and scarabs symbolising the soul or some other divine power.

We all have encoded within our psyches a map of life that goes back long before recorded history to the very beginnings of creation. There are underlying powers within us that have been disowned or forgotten with the passing of time that have to be reclaimed so that we can at last be who we really are: Gods in the making. Within our everyday existence, though we all share the same destiny, we are individuals with the gift of free will so there is no way of knowing how long it will be before we start to search in earnest for the Holy Grail, or like Don Quixote to seek 'the impossible dream', or to fight the dragons that we have created through our own lack of trust and self-awareness.

What do we need to bring us into conscious awareness? Do we need more negative witches or past black magic and self-created demons to stop our search for another few hundred years, or are we ready to be awoken by the kiss of life by a prince or the princess (which is symbolically our own divine soul)? We most certainly have the choice of agreeing to change or to remain the same for a few more lifetimes. The powers inside us can help us to unlock parts of ourselves that have hitherto remained dormant.

The **mystic** within us, for example, can empathise with the stars and understand the moods behind their twinkling light and also know how the thunder feels as it rumbles across a blackened sky. The mystic is able to connect silently with the unity of all that lives, moves and has its being in divine consciousness.

The **magician** within us (through sheer joy and divine elation) causes the sea bed to move, the angels to sing and the elemental and fairy kingdom to co-operate willingly with their need to act.

The **priest** within us links the world of the unseen with that of the seen, feeling the timeless movement of energy within the course of divine celebration, and through a deep and sacred connection purifies, blesses, makes sacred and transforms.

The power of the **warrior** is able to see without looking and know without asking; his sword symbolising his will and unconditional love as a shield, his eyes as mirrors for others to reflect upon.

The power of the **clown** is perhaps one of the most elusive yet affluent powers of all when the humour is connected to the heartbeat of sacredness. When it is divinely motivated it can fly like a golden arrow straight to the centre of the problem, making it seem funny even if the person feels that it is deadly serious, he is then able to reveal the source of his problem from a totally different perspective. The clown needs to see, know and feel what is happening behind a person's façade in order to be able to lightly crack open the self-created shell or mask, without them suffering any loss of self-respect.

These primal or archetypal powers awaken quite naturally when you connect with your own special powers. The way in which you connect with the sources of these primal powers varies somewhat as, at this stage, you are not in the process of releasing negative energies. You go through the same initial process as with Psycho-Regression, although at the bottom of the lake, well or sea you go into even deeper recesses of the self; you have the continued protection and assistance of your Guardian Angel who never leaves your side for one moment during the course of this sacred experience. When you have reached the very depths of your primal source of power, the angel is then able to create a divine illumination so that the person can clearly see the inner forms embodying the source of his or her energies. During this special time the powers that wish to make contact await the right moment for this to transpire.

The types of powers that wish to be linked with a person can be as varied as they are numerous, and can be linked with a particular area of the body, or manifest themselves within the whole psyche. Every power embodies a gift or a special quality to help the individual with whom they are connecting. A power can take any form. It may be symbolised by a dove manifesting the quality of peace, gentleness or unconditional love. There could be several power animals linked to different parts of the body or aura, such as a leopard, lion, deer or a bear, perhaps symbolising strength, stamina or affection. An eagle may be attached to the shoulders to assist the person to see situations clearly from afar, or an owl attached to the brow bringing with it the gift of wisdom.

If a person is very visual, they may see these powers strongly embodied in forms, whereas if their nature were to be more abstract they may see or feel these powers in terms of forces, precious stones or colours. As everyone is unique, so their powers manifest totally differently as they move within the elements of the earth, water, fire, air or wood. A person can link up with as many as six different types of powers at one time, more being possible, but this is enough for assimilation purposes. After receiving such unique gifts the person should not attempt to connect with any more until they feel inwardly ready to imbibe more energies into their psyche, also being objectively aware of their motives at the time. If a person is impatient or interested in power for its own sake, or if they wish to connect with these powers as a form of experiment, then they are walking a very dangerous road indeed. This is why I have repeatedly talked about the necessity for personal purification on every level, and this is why Psycho-Regression came into being.

One must not be conditioned by any preconceived idea regarding the types of power that could be encountered as they are usually very different.

A young girl saw the embodiment of her power within the form of an old woman offering her the gifts of perseverance and strength. Another person had the power manifesting itself in the form of a young boy offering the gifts of innocence and gentleness. In another the power was offered in the form of a sage, with the gifts of wisdom and learning. The person absorbs each power individually, inwardly linking it into a particular part of the body or aura before the next power comes forward. One person connected with the power of the crystal, with the gift of purification and the direction of the will, the link being attached to the frontal lobes of the brain. There could be a rainbow-coloured power attached to the whole aura and not the physical body, embodying the gifts of awareness and flexibility.

The powers are there inside each one of us to connect with, after we have first worked through our negative emotions. This part of Psycho-Regression could be likened to the icing on the birthday cake, but there is little point in the icing unless there is a beautiful, delicious cake to decorate in the first place!

I have met people during the course of my researches who consider themselves to be ceremonial magicians, but I have found many of them to be playing with energies (that are a lot more lethal than dynamite) during their magical operations, invoking all kinds of questionable spirits to their own detriment in their search for power. This causes them all sorts of unimaginable problems as they are usually convinced that is is unnecessary for them to go through the initial cleansing before putting their elevated ideas into operation. These over enthusiastic trainees of magic seem to be oblivious of the fact that when one amplifies the positive side of one's nature, the negative aspects surface simultaneously. When a person has gone through much purification, even deeper negative layers can surface as the positive side of one's nature becomes more pronounced.

There was a man who did not go through enough purification, although he thought that he had. His main fear in life was 'fear of women'. During the course of connecting with his primal powers he saw a beautiful extraterrestrial woman with large dark eyes, high cheekbones and long black hair. She wished to merge with his spirit, offering him the gift of unconditional love. Because there were residues of 'fear of women' still within his makeup, he only allowed this feminine power to merge with him from the waist upwards, and his own unresolved attitudes still affected him from the waist down. Consequently, he only benefited from this power by half, instead of in its full entirety.

A young woman had a deep 'fear of love' and when an angel of love presented itself to her wishing to connect with her spiritual heart, she immediately rejected it. This illustrates how pointless it is to attempt to connect with the source of primal power without first preparing the ground.

The purpose of connecting with these energies is to help a person to become very much more aware of who they really are, feeling and knowing, without a doubt, the source of their beginnings.

One needs to have wisdom, ability and humility to use these sacred energies constructively in the service of others and for the glory of sacredness of all life.

Creating a luminous body

We cannot effectively initiate our process of transformation until a deep inner will to change our karma emerges into consciousness. This inner resolve is strong enough to resonate within every atom and molecule of our physical bodies, creating energy waves within us that are strong enough to keep us firmly connected with our chosen course of action, also with an inner knowing that this is only possible when we have the will, energy and patience to see it through.

As we shed our unwanted karma, and gradually come to terms with past and present time ghosts, we become the initiators of our destiny. As we relinquish all of the adverse energies within us that stop us from realising our divine potential, then we become more whole or holy.

When our own consciously-directed actions are divinely motivated we are then able quite naturally to change the sub-atomic structure of the foundation of our being.

Through this inner shift of energy, a translucent luminosity starts to be emitted from the pores of the skin, like rays of light being transmitted from some heavenly domain. This sacred energy also radiates from behind the eyes, enabling us to look behind, beyond and inside the very heart of man. Such eyes are able to know and to understand man and womankind's needs, joys, sorrows and deepest aspirations. A luminescent being who has shed the heavy encumbrance of the personality feels lighter and far more flexible, and therefore quite at home in all domains, as he or she is not limited by personal projections or short-sighted wants and desires.

A luminescent being or enlightened one is able to communicate with all aspects of life, moving with ease from minutes to days, to months, to years, on to millennia. These beings are able to communicate freely with the spirits of past saints and sinners of this world without limitations of judgement, and to enter into telepathic discourse with philosophers and scientists who have long gone from this earth, and who wholeheartedly share their sacred knowledge with those who are willing to receive it. All of this and more is possible for a person who initiates his or her own path of destiny, a person who is really willing to look for and to find the God-within.

CONCLUSION

During my life I have met people who have, to a greater or lesser extent, been able to communicate with the God-within. I have seen it with my eyes, felt it in my heart and many times I have seen divinity actively manifesting itself in many different ways. I know without a shadow of doubt that a person can bring about great inner changes when they are inwardly motivated to do so. The information in this book is not based on intellectual theory or speculation, it is from experience and research based on many people's individual realities over a 20-year period, also information channelled through me telepathically from other dimensions of intellect. This work not only succinctly covers a very unique brand of regression, it also encompasses so much more in its wake, revealing to the reader many unusual facets of multi-dimensional healing.

Psycho-Regression is one of the most comprehensive systems in the Western hemisphere to deal with so many intricate and sometimes complex aspects of the human psyche in a detailed and systematic way, at the same time leaving plenty of room for the divine energies to flow unimpeded through the whole sacred procedure. There are also many invisible beings available to enable it all to flow according to the divine plan.

The attributes of a practitioner for this unusual type of work are the need to be physically fit as well as spiritually dedicated, and they also need to be flexible and compassionate.

It is possible to train suitable people, who have been inspired by this book and are wanting to learn more about this unique therapy and who have an instinctive understanding of this type of work, with perhaps a therapeutic or healing background to help them along their chosen path.

Ideally it would be good to have practitioners available from many different cultures throughout the world. I would like to find sufficient mature people with plenty of physical and spiritual stamina, who are really willing to take this long but hard and rewarding journey. I would then consider this to be a very positive step in the right direction for both the trainee and the people they will be treating, as both will inwardly benefit from doing this work.

Twelve well-trained practitioners who are also capable of teaching could train many more. People have made the initial mistake of thinking that anyone can do this therapy after just a few seminars. However, the course takes three years of part-time studies and practice to learn, through observation and understanding the mechanics of the therapy, personal spiritual development and purifi-cation, to the receiving of therapy as well as practising it under the watchful eye of a qualified practitioner.

I have listed details of practitioners and various methods of spiritual purification at the end of this book. At the time of writing the book, there are only a few fully trained

Psycho-Regression therapists in England and only one in the USA.

I have treated patients over the last 20 years and now I have reduced this aspect of my work in order to teach the therapy and to write on the research and discoveries that I have made during my time as a practitioner.

I know that this therapy can help many different types of people, including those who have an inner belief in something, but maybe are not quite sure what that 'something' is. If there are enough spiritually orientated people with a therapeutic background or a good knowledge of healing who are willing to learn this work, then a great deal could really be achieved.

Psycho-Regression is a valid path to finding the God-within. The mountain can be steep and hazardous, though it is breathtakingly beautiful.

We really do need to know ourselves, and this is one excellent way of making that discovery.

GLOSSARY

Abhyasi: Aspirant; one who practises yoga in order to achieve communion with God.

Angels: Divine messengers, communicating/functioning between God and man.

Guardian Angels: A Guardian spirit, personal protector.

Aura: Subtle emanation surrounding the physical body (depth and colour varies according to the person's spiritual growth and physical energy).

Biodynamic Massage: A form of massage that releases blocked emotions within the tissues and muscles, bringing the whole being into balance.

Cells: Unit of structure of living matter containing a nucleus.

Chakras: In Sanskrit, chakra means wheel. They are energy points in the astral body. Chakra development indicates the state of psychic development. In a meditative state the chakras open up like beautiful flowers.

Deific: Godlike in form or nature.

Devolution: Opposite to evolution. To go down. Destruction.

Evolution: Unfolding. Development. Spiritual growth.

Gnostic: Having superior knowledge of spiritual mysteries.

Illumination: Spiritual and intellectual light. (At one with God.)

Inter-life: Life between life. (See Further Reading)

Karma: Fate, destiny (as determined by one's actions in a former state of existence).

Medicine Man/Woman: A person with the art of preserving and restoring health (in a natural way).

Primal Powers: Origin. Source of power.

Psyche: The soul, spirit, mind.

Psychic: Senses outside of the physical domain.

Genetics: Pertaining to origin.

Psychic-Genetics: Origin of our psychic make-up.

Psychic Injuries: Injuries to our psychic make-up, past or present (remaining in the very cells of the psyche).

Psycho: Relating to the psyche.

Physical Genetics: Origin of our physical make-up.

Psychic Skin Structure: Invisible covering over the skin.

Incarnation: Embodiment in flesh.

Reincarnation: To incarnate again into another body.

Shaman: A person who can change his consciousness at will and travel into other dimensions. (May also be a priest/healer or medicine man/woman.)

Sub-personalities: Unintegrated past personalities which are deeply embedded in the subconscious.

Transformation: Changing the form of . . .

SUGGESTED READING

Alder, V. S. *The Finding of the Third Eye*. York Beach, ME: Samuel Weiser, 1970; and London: Rider, 1962.

Ashley, N. *Create Your Own Reality: A Seth Workbook*. New York: Prentice Hall, a Division of Simon & Schuster, 1987.

Aivanhov, O. M. *Man's Subtle Bodies and Centres*. Los Angeles: Prosveta, 1986.

Bach, E. *Heal Thyself*. Saffron Walden, UK: C. W. Daniel, 1988.

Boericke, W. and Oscar E. *Homeopathic and Materia Medica*. Kent, UK: Homeopathic Book Service, 1990.

Brennan, B. A. *Hands of Light*. New York: Bantam, 1988.

Chandra, Ram. *The Complete Works of Ram Chandra*, Vols. I and II. France: Ram Chandra Mission, 1989.

Conger, J. P. *Jung and Reich: The Body as Shadow*. Berkeley, CA: North Atlantic, 1988.

Danielou, Jean S. J. *The Angels and their Mission*. Dublin: Four Courts Press, 1988.

Edwards, Gill. *Living Magically*. London: Piatkus, 1991.

Fisher, J. *The Case of Reincarnation*. Secaucus, NJ: Carol Publishing Group, 1992.

Grant, D. and J. Joice. *Food Combining for Health*. Rochester, VT: Inner Traditions, 1987.

Grant, J. and D. Kelsey. *Many Lifetimes*. London: Gollancz, 1968.

Guirdham, A. *Cosmic Factors in Disease*. London: Duckworth, 1963.

———. *The Psyche in Medicine*. Saffron Walden, UK: Neville Spearman, 1978.

———. *The Psychic Dimensions of Mental Health*. London: Turnstone Press, a division of HarperCollins, 1982.

———. *A Theory of Disease*. Saffron Walden, UK: Neville Spearman, 1957.

Gullan-Whur, M. *The Four Elements*. London: Century, 1987.

Gris, H. and Dick W. *The New Soviet Psychic Discoveries*. London: Souvenir Press, 1978.

Gurudas. *Gem Elixers and Vibrational Healing*, Vols. I and II. San Rafael, CA: Cassandra Press, 1989.

Hall, Manley P. *Man The Grand Symbol of the Mysteries*. Los Angeles: Philosophical Research, 1932.

Hay, L. *Heal Your Body*. Carson, CA: Hay House; London: Eden Grove, 1988.

Jung, Dr. C. G. *Modern Man in Search of a Soul*. New York: Harcourt Brace, 1955.

———. *Symbols of Transformation*, volume 5 of *The Collected Works of C. G. Jung*, translated by R. F. C. Hull, Bollingen Series XX. Princeton, NJ: Princeton University Press, 1956; and London: Routledge & Kegan Paul, 1967.

King, S. *Magic of Angels*. London: Seekers Trust, 1979.

Krippners, S. and D. Rubin. *The Kirlain Aura*. New York: Anchor, 1974.

Krystal, P. *Cutting the Ties that Bind*. York Beach, ME: Samuel Weiser, 1993; originally published by Sawbridge Press, UK, 1983.

Leadbeater, C. W. *The Chakras*. Wheaton, IL: Quest Books, 1972.

Mallasz, G. *Talking with Angels*. London: Watkins, 1979.

Mees, L. F. C. *Secrets of the Skeleton*. Spring Valley, NY: Anthroposophic Press, 1984.

Mickaharic, D. *Spiritual Cleansing*. York Beach, ME: Samuel Weiser, 1982; also published as *Handbook of Psychic Protection*, London: Rider, 1992.

Motoyama, Dr. Hiroshi. *Karma and Reincarnation*. London: Piatkus, 1992.

Naegeli-Osjord, H. M. D. *Possession and Exorcism*. USA: New Frontiers Center, 1988.

Nicholson, S. *Shamanism*. Wheaton, IL: Quest Books, 1988.

Oesterreich, T. K. *Possession: Demoniacal and Other*. Secaucus, NJ: Carol Publishing Group, 1974; and London: Kegan Paul, 1930.

Pierrakos, Dr. J. *Core Energetics*. Mendocino, CA: Life Rhythm Publications, 1987.

Proto, L. *Who's Pulling Your Strings?* London: Thorsons, a division of HarperCollins, 1989.

Rowan, J. *Subpersonalities*. London: Routledge, 1990.

Sargant, Wm. *The Mind Possessed*. London: Heinemann, 1973.

Sandner, D. *Navaho Symbols of Healing*. Rochester, VT: Healing Arts Press, a division of Inner Traditions, 1979.

Thighten, C. H. *The Three Faces of Eve*. Bath, UK: Chivers, 1985.

Valliereres, I. *Reincarnation Therapy*. Bath, UK: Ashgrove Press, 1991.

Walker, K. *Diagnosis of Man*. Gretna, LA: Pelican Books, 1962.

Wheeler, F. J. *The Bach Remedies Repertory*. Saffron Walden, UK: C. W. Daniel, 1973.

Whitten, Dr. J. L. and J. Fisher. *Life Between Life*. London: Grafton Books, 1986.

Williston, G. and J. Johnstone. *Soul Search*. London: Turnstone Press, a division of HarperCollins, 1983.

Wilson, P. L. *Angels*. London: Thames & Hudson, 1990.

RESOURCES

Please send a SASE or international reply coupons for all queries.

Dr. Francesca Rossetti
The Rossetti Foundation
B/M Spiritos
London WC1N 3XX
England
Lecturer, teacher on Psycho-Regression and other therapies.
Also a para-medical researcher.

Jane Swaan
RR1 Box 640
Bradford, VT 05033-9711
USA
Psycho-Regression,
Pre-Creation (Soul Therapy)

Dr. S. Srivastava
Kanupriya
Sri Ram Chandrapuram
Kheri Road
Lakhimpur-Kheri 262701
India
Sahaj Marg
System of Meditation

Ram Chandra Mission
Chateau D'Augerans
39380 Mont Sous
Vaudray
France
Sahaj Marg
System of Meditation

The Rossetti Foundation
B/M Spiritos
London WC1N 3XX
England
Sahaj Marg System (clearing karma through spiritual transmissions and meditation) and also for list of Sahaj Marg preceptors in the UK

The Seekers Trust
The Close
Addington Park
West Malling
Kent ME19 5BL
England
Centre for prayer and spiritual healing. Through this centre it is possible to receive long distance spiritual healing, assisted by the angels.

Jenai Cotteril
B/M Devi
London WC1N 3XX
England
Psycho-Regression,
Pre-Creation (Soul Therapy),
Bio-Dynamic Massage

INDEX

Dr. Francesca Rossetti is an international lecturer, author, para-medical researcher, and spiritual teacher. Her knowledge and ability to understand people and their complexities comes from over twenty years experience as a therapist and healer. Through her many years of research, she has devised two of the most important therapies for the new age: Pre-Creation (Soul Therapy) and Psycho-Regression Therapy. While Pre-Creation Therapy helps to release the primal causes of physical and emotional imbalances without actually having to regress into the trauma, Psycho-Regression Therapy enables the person to regress to the primal cause, as well as release the emotions connected with the trauma. Rossetti works with people who seek to awaken the slumbering God within the physical body, through spiritual discipline, prayer, meditation, and awakening of the heart center through various processes of spiritual development. She lives and works in London.